Published by Brighter Child®
an imprint of Carson-Dellosa Publishing LLC
Greensboro, NC

Brighter Child®
An imprint of Carson-Dellosa Publishing LLC
P.O. Box 35665
Greensboro, NC 27425 USA

© 2006 Carson-Dellosa Publishing LLC. Except as permitted under the United States Copyright Act, no part of this publication may be reproduced, stored, or distributed in any form or by any means (mechanically, electronically, recording, etc.) without the prior written consent of Carson-Dellosa Publishing LLC. Brighter Child® is an imprint of Carson-Dellosa Publishing LLC.

Printed in the USA • All rights reserved. ISBN 0-7696-7625-1

07-202147784

Table of Contents

Brighter Child
English and Grammar
Grade 5

 ©2006 Carson-Dellosa Publishing

Name ______________________________

Nouns

A **noun** is a word that names a person, place or thing.

Examples:
person — friend
place — home
thing — desk

Nouns are used many ways in sentences. They can be the subjects of sentences.

Example: Noun as subject: Your high-topped **sneakers** look great with that outfit.

Nouns can be direct objects of a sentence. The **direct object** follows the verb and completes its meaning. It answers the question **who** or **what**.

Example: Noun as direct object: Shelly's family bought a new **car**.

Nouns can be indirect objects. An **indirect object** comes between the verb and the direct object and tells **to whom** or **for whom** something was done.

Example: Noun as indirect object: She gave **Tina** a big hug.

Directions: Underline all the nouns. Write **S** above the noun if it is a subject, **DO** if it is a direct object or **IO** if it is an indirect object. The first one has been done for you.

1. Do alligators (S) eat people (DO)?
2. James hit a home run, and our team won the game.
3. The famous actor gave Susan his autograph.
4. Eric loaned Keith his bicycle.
5. The kindergarten children painted cute pictures.
6. Robin sold David some chocolate chip cookies.
7. The neighbors planned a going-away party and bought a gift.
8. The party and gift surprised Kurt and his family.
9. My scout leader told our group a funny joke.
10. Karen made her little sister a clown costume.

Name ______________________________

Proper and Common Nouns

Proper nouns name specific people, places or things.

Examples: Washington, D.C., Thomas Jefferson, Red Sea

Common nouns name nonspecific people, places or things.

Examples: man, fortress, dog

Directions: Underline the proper nouns and circle the common nouns in each sentence.

1. My friend, Josephine, loves to go to the docks to watch the boats sail into the harbor.
2. Josephine is especially interested in the boat named *Maiden Voyage*.
3. This boat is painted red with yellow stripes and has several large masts.
4. Its sails are white and billow in the wind.
5. At Misty Harbor, many boats are always sailing in and out.
6. The crews on the boats rush from bow to stern working diligently to keep the sailboats moving.
7. Josephine has been invited aboard *Maiden Voyage* by its captain.
8. Captain Ferdinand knew of her interest in sailboats, so he offered a tour.
9. Josephine was amazed at the gear aboard the boat and the skills of the crew.
10. It is Josephine's dream to sail the Atlantic Ocean on a boat similar to *Maiden Voyage*.
11. Her mother is not sure of this dangerous dream and urges Josephine to consider safer dreams.
12. Josephine thinks of early explorers like Christopher Columbus, Amerigo Vespucci and Leif Ericson.
13. She thinks these men must have been brave to set out into the unknown waters of the world.
14. Their boats were often small and provided little protection from major ocean storms.
15. Josephine believes that if early explorers could challenge the rough ocean waters, she could, too.

©2006 Carson-Dellosa Publishing

Name ______________________________

Abstract and Concrete Nouns

Concrete nouns name something that can be touched or seen. **Abstract nouns** name an idea, a thought or a feeling which cannot be touched or seen.

Examples:
concrete nouns: house, puppy, chair
abstract nouns: love, happiness, fear

Directions: Write **concrete** or **abstract** in the blank after each noun.

1. loyalty a
2. light bulb c
3. quarter c
4. hope a
5. satellite c
6. ability a
7. patio c
8. door c
9. allegiance a
10. Cuba c
11. Michael Jordan c
12. friendship a
13. telephone c
14. computer c

Directions: Write eight nouns for each category.

Concrete	Abstract
1. phone	1. Love
2.	2. Kindness
3.	3. sadness
4.	4. freedom
5.	5. fearful
6.	6. worry
7.	7.
8.	8.

Name ______________________

Verbs

A **verb** tells what something does or that something exists.

Examples:

Tim **has shared** his apples with us.
Those apples **were** delicious.
I hope Tim **is bringing** more apples tomorrow.
Tim **picked** the apples himself.

Directions: Underline the verbs.

1. Gene moved here from Philadelphia.
2. Now he is living in a house on my street.
3. His house is three houses away from mine.
4. I have lived in this house all my life.
5. I hope Gene will like this town.
6. I am helping Gene with his room.
7. He has a lot of stuff!
8. We are painting his walls green.
9. He picked the color himself.
10. I wonder what his parents will say.

Directions: Write verbs to complete these sentences.

11. We ______________________ some paint brushes.
12. Gene already ______________________ the paint.
13. I ______________________ my old clothes.
14. There ______________________ no furniture in his room right now.
15. It ______________________ several hours to paint his whole room.

©2006 Carson-Dellosa Publishing

Name ______________________

Verb Tenses

Verbs have different forms to show whether something already happened, is happening right now or will happen.

Examples:

Present tense: I **walk**.
Past tense: I **walked**.
Future tense: I **will walk**.

Directions: Write **PAST** if the verb is past tense, **PRES** for present tense or **FUT** for future tense. The first one has been done for you.

PRES 1. My sister Sara works at the grocery store.

_______ 2. Last year, she worked in an office.

_______ 3. Sara is going to college, too.

_______ 4. She will be a dentist some day.

_______ 5. She says studying is difficult.

_______ 6. Sara hardly studied at all in high school.

_______ 7. I will be ready for college in a few years.

_______ 8. Last night, I read my history book for 2 hours.

Directions: Complete these sentences using verbs in the tenses listed. The first one has been done for you.

9. take: future tense — My friends and I will take a trip.
10. talk: past tense — We ____________ for a long time about where to go.
11. want: present tense — Pam ____________ to go to the lake.
12. want: past tense — Jake ____________ to go with us.
13. say: past tense — His parents ____________ no.
14. ride: future tense — We ____________ our bikes.
15. pack: past tense — Susan and Jared already ____________ lunches for us.

©2006 Carson-Dellosa Publishing

Name ______________________

Verb Tenses

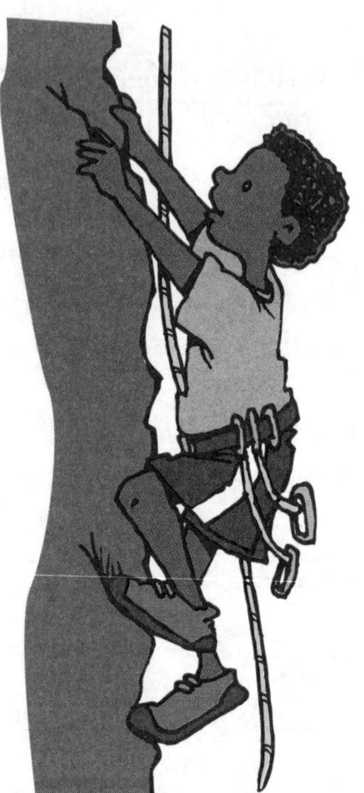

The past tense of many verbs is formed by adding **ed**.

Examples:

remember + **ed** = remembered
climb + **ed** = climbed

If a verb ends in **e**, drop the **e** before adding **ed**.

Examples:

Present	**Past**
phone	phoned
arrive	arrived

If a verb ends in **y**, change the **y** to **i** before adding **ed**.

Examples:

Present	**Past**
carry	carried
try	tried

If a verb ends in a short vowel followed by a single consonant, double the final consonant.

Examples:

Present	**Past**
trip	tripped
pop	popped

Directions: Circle the misspelled verb in each sentence and write it correctly in the blank.

1. They stopped at our house and then hurryed home. ______________
2. I scrubed and mopped the floor. ______________
3. The coach nameed the five starting players. ______________
4. He popped the potatoes into the oil and fryed them. ______________
5. I accidentally droped my papers on the floor. ______________
6. I had hopeed you could could go climbing with me. ______________
7. He triped on the rug. ______________
8. The baby cryed and screamed all night. ______________
9. I moped the mess up after the glass dropped on the floor. ______________
10. First, she frowned, and then she smileed. ______________

 ©2006 Carson-Dellosa Publishing

Name ______________________________

Principal Parts of Verbs

Verbs have three principal parts. They are **present**, **past** and **past participle**.

Regular verbs form the past tense by adding **ed** to the present tense.

The past participle is formed by using the past tense verb with a helping verb: **has**, **have** or **had**.

Directions: Write the correct form of each verb. The first one has been done for you.

Present	Past	Past Participle
1. look	looked	have/has/had looked
2. ______	planned	______
3. ______	______	has/have/had closed
4. wash	______	______
5. ______	prepared	______
6. ______	______	has/have/had provided
7. invite	______	______
8. ______	discovered	______
9. approve	______	______
10. ______	searched	______
11. establish	______	______
12. ______	______	has/have/had formed
13. ______	pushed	______
14. travel	______	______

©2006 Carson-Dellosa Publishing

Name ____________________

Irregular Verbs

Irregular verbs change completely in the past tense. Unlike regular verbs, the past tense forms of irregular verbs are not formed by adding **ed**.

Examples:

Chung **eats** the cookies.
Chung **ate** them yesterday.
Chung **has eaten** them for weeks.

Present Tense	Past Tense	Past Participle
begin	began	has/have/had begun
speak	spoke	has/have/had spoken
drink	drank	has/have/had drunk
know	knew	has/have/had known
eat	ate	has/have/had eaten
wear	wore	has/have/had worn

Directions: Rewrite these sentences once using the past tense and again using the past participle of each verb.

1. Todd begins football practice this week.

____

____

2. She wears her hair in braids.

____

____

3. I drink two glasses of milk.

____

____

4. The man is speaking to us.

____

____

5. The dogs are eating.

____

____

 ©2006 Carson-Dellosa Publishing

Name ______________________

Irregular Verbs

The past participle form of an irregular verb needs a helping verb.

Examples:

Present	**Past**	**Past Participle**
begin	began	has/have/had begun
drive	drove	has/have/had driven

Directions: Write the past and past participle form of these irregular verbs. Use a dictionary if you need help.

Present	Past	Past Participle
1. speak	______________	______________
2. break	______________	______________
3. beat	______________	______________
4. dream	______________	______________
5. tear	______________	______________
6. forget	______________	______________
7. lead	______________	______________
8. stand	______________	______________
9. sting	______________	______________
10. freeze	______________	______________
11. grow	______________	______________
12. lose	______________	______________
13. run	______________	______________
14. meet	______________	______________
15. sit	______________	______________
16. do	______________	______________

Name ______________________________

"Be" as a Helping Verb

A **helping verb** tells when the action of a sentence takes place. The helping verb **be** has several forms: **am**, **is**, **are**, **was**, **were** and **will**. These helping verbs can be used in all three tenses.

Examples:

Past tense: Ken **was** talking. We **were** eating.
Present tense: I **am** coming. Simon **is** walking. They **are** singing.
Future tense: I **will** work. The puppies **will** eat.

In the present and past tense, many verbs can be written with or without the helping verb **be**. When the verb is written with a form of **be**, add **ing**. **Was** and **is** are used with singular subjects. **Were** and **are** are used with plural subjects.

Examples:

Present tense: Angela **sings**. Angela **is singing**. The children **sing**. They **are singing**.
Past tense: I **studied**. I **was studying**. They **studied**. They **were studying**.

The helping verb **will** is always needed for the future tense, but the **ing** ending is not used with **will**. **Will** is both singular and plural.

Examples:

Future tense: I **will eat**. We **will watch**.

Directions: Underline the helping verbs.

1. Brian is helping me with this project.
2. We are working together on it.
3. Susan was painting the background yesterday.
4. Matt and Mike were cleaning up.
5. Tomorrow, we will present our project to the class.

Directions: Rewrite the verbs using a helping verb. The first one has been done for you.

6. Our neighborhood plans a garage sale. ______is planning______
7. The sale starts tomorrow. ______________________
8. My brother Doug and I think about things we sell. ______________________
9. My grandfather cleans out the garage. ______________________
10. Doug and I help him. ______________________

 ©2006 Carson-Dellosa Publishing

Name ______________________________

"Be" as a Linking Verb

A **linking verb** links a noun or adjective in the predicate to the subject. Forms of the verb **be** are the most common linking verbs. Linking verbs can be used in all three tenses.

Examples:

Present: My father **is** a salesman.
Past: The store **was** very busy last night.
Future: Tomorrow **will be** my birthday.

In the first sentence, **is** links the subject (father) with a noun (salesman). In the second sentence, **was** links the subject (store) with an adjective (busy). In the third sentence, **will be** links the subject (tomorrow) with a noun (birthday).

Directions: Circle the linking verbs. Underline the two words that are linked by the verb. The first one has been done for you.

1. Columbus (is) the capital of Ohio.
2. By bedtime, Nicole was bored.
3. Andy will be the captain of our team.
4. Tuesday is the first day of the month.
5. I hate to say this, but we are lost.
6. Ask him if the water is cold.
7. By the time I finished my paper, it was late.
8. Spaghetti is my favorite dinner.
9. The children were afraid of the big truck.
10. Karen will be a good president of our class.
11. These lessons are helpful.
12. Was that report due today?

Name ________________________

Direct Objects

A **direct object** is a word or words that follow a transitive verb and complete its meaning. It answers the question **who** or **what**. Direct objects are always nouns or pronouns.

Examples:

We built a **doghouse**. **Doghouse** is the direct object. It tells **what** we built.
I called **Mary**. **Mary** is the direct object. It tells **who** I called.

Directions: Underline the direct objects.

1. Jean drew a picture of the doghouse.
2. Then we bought some wood at the store.
3. Erin measured each board.
4. Who will saw the wood into boards?
5. Chad hammered nails into the boards.
6. He accidentally hit his thumb with the hammer.
7. Kirsten found some paint in the basement.
8. Should we paint the roof?
9. Will you write Sparky's name above the door?
10. Spell his name correctly.

Directions: Write direct objects to complete these sentences.

11. Will Sparky like ________________________?
12. When we were finished, we put away ________________________.
13. We washed out ________________________.
14. We threw away ________________________.
15. Then, to celebrate, we ate ________________________.

 ©2006 Carson-Dellosa Publishing

Name ______________________________

Indirect Objects

An **indirect object** is a word or words that come between the verb and the direct object. An indirect object tells **to whom** or **for whom** something has been done. Indirect objects are always nouns or pronouns.

Examples:

She cooked **me** a great dinner. **Me** is the indirect object. It tells **for whom** something was cooked.

Give the **photographer** a smile. **Photographer** is the indirect object. It tells **to whom** the smile should be given.

Directions: Circle the indirect objects. Underline the direct objects.

1. Marla showed me her drawing.
2. The committee had given her an award for it.
3. The principal offered Marla a special place to put her drawing.
4. While babysitting, I read Timmy a story.
5. He told me the end of the story.
6. Then I fixed him some hot chocolate.
7. Timmy gave me a funny look.
8. Why didn't his mother tell me?
9. Hot chocolate gives Timmy a rash.
10. Will his mom still pay me three dollars for watching him?

Directions: Write indirect objects to complete these sentences.

11. I will write ______________________________ a letter.
12. I'll give ______________________________ part of my lunch.
13. Show ______________________________ your model.
14. Did you send ______________________________ a card?
15. Don't tell ______________________________ my secret.

©2006 Carson-Dellosa Publishing

Name ______________________________

Subjects and Predicates

The **subject** tells who or what a sentence is about. The **predicate** tells what the subject does, did or is doing. All complete sentences must have a subject and a predicate.

Examples:

Subject	**Predicate**
Hamsters	are common pets.
Pets	need special care.

Directions: Circle the subjects and underline the predicates.

1. Many children keep hamsters as pets.
2. Mice are good pets, too.
3. Hamsters collect food in their cheeks.
4. My sister sneezes around furry animals.
5. My brother wants a dog instead of a hamster.

Directions: Write subjects to complete these sentences.

6. ____________________ has two pet hamsters.
7. ____________________ got a new pet last week.
8. ____________________ keeps forgetting to feed his goldfish.

Directions: Write predicates to complete these sentences.

9. Baby hamsters ____.
10. Pet mice ____.
11. I ____.

Directions: Write **S** if the group of words is a sentence or **NS** if the group of words is not a sentence.

12. ____________________ A new cage for our hamster.
13. ____________________ Picked the cutest one.
14. ____________________ We started out with two.
15. ____________________ Liking every one in the store.

 ©2006 Carson-Dellosa Publishing

Name ______________________________

Complete Sentences

A sentence which does not contain both a subject and a predicate is called a **fragment**.

Directions: Write **C** if the sentence is complete or **F** if it is a fragment.

1. ________ My mother and I hope to go to the mall this afternoon.
2. ________ To get shoes.
3. ________ We both need a new pair of tennis shoes.
4. ________ Maybe blue and white.
5. ________ Mom wants a pair of white shoes.
6. ________ That seems rather boring to me.
7. ________ There are many shoe stores in the mall.
8. ________ Sure to be a large selection.
9. ________ Tennis shoes are very expensive.
10. ________ My last pair cost $72.00!

Directions: Write the missing subject or predicate for these sentences.

11. ______________________________ decided to go for hamburgers.
12. We ______________________________.
13. My parents ______________________________.
14. One day soon, I ______________________________.
15. My favorite subject in school ______________________________.
16. ______________________________ went fishing on Sunday.

Name ______________________________

Pronouns as Subjects

A **pronoun** is a word that takes the place of a noun. The pronouns **I**, **we**, **he**, **she**, **it**, **you** and **they** can be the subjects of a sentence.

Examples:

I left the house early.
You need to be more careful.
She dances well.

A pronoun must be singular if the noun it replaces is singular. A pronoun must be plural if the noun it replaces is plural. **He**, **she** and **it** are singular pronouns. **We** and **they** are plural pronouns. **You** is both singular and plural.

Examples:

Tina practiced playing the piano. **She** plays well.
Jim and I are studying Africa. **We** made a map of it.
The children clapped loudly. **They** liked the clown.

Directions: Write the correct pronouns.

1. Bobcats hunt at night. ________________ are not seen during the day.
2. The mother bobcat usually has babies during February or March. ________________ may have two litters a year.
3. The father bobcat stays away when the babies are first born. Later, ________________ helps find food for them.
4. We have a new assignment. ________________ is a project about bobcats.
5. My group gathered pictures of bobcats. ________________ made a display.
6. Jennifer wrote our report. ________________ used my notes.

Directions: Circle the pronouns that do not match the nouns they replace. Then write the correct pronouns on the lines.

7. Two boys saw a bobcat. He told us what happened. ________________
8. Then we saw a film. They showed bobcats climbing trees. ________________

 ©2006 Carson-Dellosa Publishing

Name ______________________________

Prepositions

A **preposition** is a word that comes before a noun or pronoun and shows the relationship of that noun or pronoun to other words in the sentence.

The **object of a preposition** is a noun or pronoun that follows a preposition and completes its meaning. A **prepositional phrase** includes a preposition and the object(s) of the preposition.

Examples:

The girl **with red hair** spoke first.
With is the preposition.
Hair is the object of the preposition.
With red hair is a prepositional phrase.

In addition to being subjects, direct and indirect objects, nouns and pronouns can also be objects of prepositions.

Prepositions

across	below	from	near	over	to	on
by	through	in	under	off	with	of
after	before	for	between	beyond	at	down

Directions: Underline the prepositional phrases in these sentences. Circle the prepositions. The first sentence has been done for you.

1. The name (of) <u>of our street</u> is Redsail Court.
2. We have lived in our house for three years.
3. In our family, we eat a lot of hamburgers.
4. We like hamburgers on toasted buns with mustard.
5. Sometimes we eat in the living room in front of the TV.
6. In the summer, we have picnics in the backyard.
7. The ants crawl into our food and into our clothes.
8. Behind our house is a park with swings.
9. Kids from the neighborhood walk through our yard to the park.
10. Sometimes they cut across Mom's garden and stomp on her beans.
11. Mom says we need a tall fence without a gate.
12. With a fence around our yard, we could get a dog!

Name ______________________

Gender and Number of Pronouns

Pronouns that identify males are **masculine gender**. The masculine pronouns are **he**, **his** and **him**. Pronouns that identify females are **feminine gender**. The feminine pronouns are **she**, **her** and **hers**. Pronouns that identify something that is neither male nor female are **neuter gender**. The neuter pronouns are **it** and **its**.

The plural pronouns **they** and **them** are used for masculine, feminine or neuter gender.

Examples:

Noun	**Pronoun**	**Noun**	**Pronoun**
boot	it	woman	she
man	he	John's	his
travelers	they	dog's	its

Directions: List four nouns that each pronoun could replace in a sentence. The first one has been done for you.

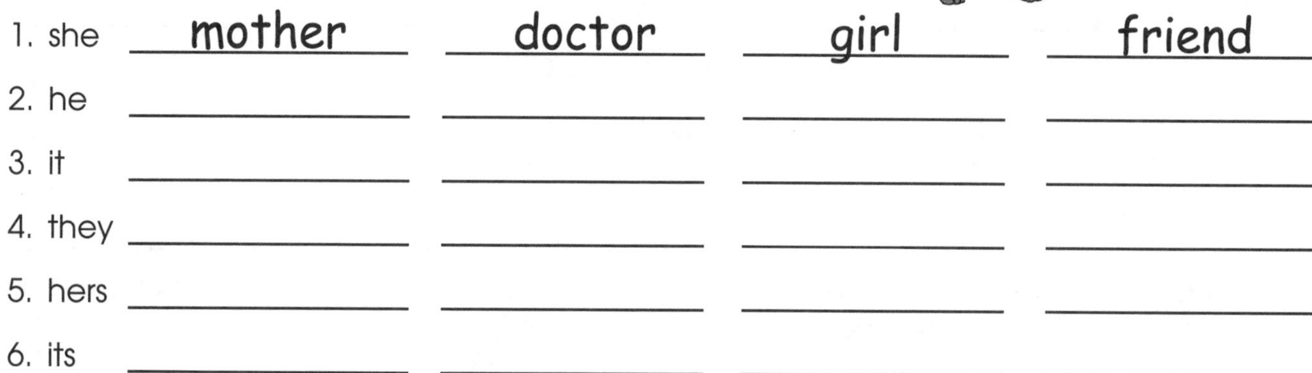

1. she ___mother___ ___doctor___ ___girl___ ___friend___
2. he ________ ________ ________ ________
3. it ________ ________ ________ ________
4. they ________ ________ ________ ________
5. hers ________ ________ ________ ________
6. its ________ ________ ________ ________

Singular pronouns take the place of singular nouns. Plural pronouns take the place of plural nouns. The singular pronouns are **I**, **me**, **mine**, **he**, **she**, **it**, **its**, **hers**, **his**, **him**, **her**, **you** and **yours**. The plural pronouns are **we**, **you**, **yours**, **they**, **theirs**, **ours**, **them** and **us**.

Directions: Write five sentences. Include a singular and a plural pronoun in each sentence.

1. ______________________________
2. ______________________________
3. ______________________________
4. ______________________________
5. ______________________________

 ©2006 Carson-Dellosa Publishing

Name ______________________________

Possessive Pronouns

A **possessive pronoun** shows ownership. A possessive pronoun can be used with the name of what is owned or by itself.

Examples:

This **my** book. The book is **mine**.
This is **your** sandwich. It is **yours**.
This is **our** room. The room is **ours**.

The possessive pronouns are **my**, **your**, **our**, **his**, **her**, **their**, **its**, **mine**, **yours**, **ours**, **hers** and **theirs**. Possessive pronouns do not have apostrophes.

Directions: Complete the sentences with the correct possessive pronouns.

1. I entered ____________ picture in the contest. That farm scene is ______________.
2. Shelby entered ____________ picture, too. Do you see _______________?
3. Hal didn't finish ____________ drawing. He left ______________ at home.
4. Did you enter ______________ clay pot? That looks like _______________.
5. One picture has fallen off ______________ stand.
6. Brian and Kendell worked together on a chalk drawing. That sketch by the doorway is _______________.
7. The judges have made _______________ choices.
8. We both won! They picked both of _______________!
9. Here come the judges with our ribbons in ________________ hands.
10. Your ribbon is the same as _________________.

Name ______________________________

Pronouns

Subjects:	he	she	it	you	I	they	we
Objects:	him	her	it	you	me	them	us
Possessive:	his	her	its	your	my	their	our
Possessive:	his	hers	its	yours	mine	theirs	ours
Indefinite:	everyone	nobody	something	(and others)			

Directions: Complete these sentences with the correct pronouns from the box. Above each pronoun, write how it is used: **S** for subject, **DO** for direct object, **IO** for indirect object, **OP** for object of a preposition, **PP** for possessive pronoun or **IP** for indefinite pronoun.

1. Last week, we had a food drive at ____________________ church.
2. ____________________ in our Sunday school class helped collect food.
3. I walked down my street and asked ____________________ neighbors for food.
4. They gave ____________________ cans and boxes of food.
5. Kelly came with ______________ and helped ______________carry all of ___________.
6. Paul had brought his old red wagon from ____________________ house.
7. When I saw it, ____________________ wished I had brought ____________________.
8. Kelly and ____________________ had to put ____________________ cans in grocery bags.
9. Those bags were really heavy when ____________________ were full.
10. When I picked one up, ____________________ tore and the cans fell out!
11. Jeremy's sister gave ____________________ a ride around the neighborhood.
12. Walking made Kelly and ____________________ hungry.

 ©2006 Carson-Dellosa Publishing

Name ______________________________

Conjunctions

A **conjunction** joins words or groups of words in a sentence. The most commonly used conjunctions are **and**, **but** and **or**.

Examples: My brother **and** I each want to win the trophy.
Tonight, it will rain **or** sleet.
I wanted to go to the party, **but** I got sick.

Directions: Circle the conjunctions.

1. Dolphins and whales are mammals.
2. They must rise to the surface of the water to breathe, or they will die.
3. Dolphins resemble fish, but they are not fish.
4. Sightseeing boats are often entertained by groups of dolphins or whales.
5. Whales appear to effortlessly leap out of the water and execute flips.
6. Both whale and dolphin babies are born alive.
7. The babies are called calves and are born in the water, but must breathe air within a few minutes of birth.
8. Sometimes an entire pod of whales will help a mother and calf reach the surface to breathe.
9. Scientists and marine biologists have long been intrigued by these ocean animals.
10. Whales and dolphins do not seem to be afraid of humans or boats.

Directions: Write six sentences using conjunctions.

11. ______________________________
12. ______________________________
13. ______________________________
14. ______________________________
15. ______________________________
16. ______________________________

Name ______________________

Compound Subjects/Compound Predicates

A **compound subject** has two or more nouns or pronouns joined by a conjunction. Compound subjects share the same predicate.

Examples:

Suki and Spot walked to the park in the rain.
Cars, buses and trucks splashed water on them.
He and I were glad we had our umbrella.

A **compound predicate** has two or more verbs joined by a conjunction. Compound predicates share the same subject.

Examples:

Suki **went** in the restroom **and wiped** off her shoes.
Paula **followed** Suki **and waited** for her.

A sentence can have a compound subject and a compound predicate.

Example: Tina and Maria went to the mall **and shopped** for an hour.

Directions: Circle the compound subjects. Underline the compound predicates.

1. Steve and Jerry went to the store and bought some gum.
2. Police and firefighters worked together and put out the fire.
3. Karen and Marsha did their homework and checked it twice.
4. In preschool, the boys and girls drew pictures and colored them.

Directions: Write compound subjects to go with these predicates.

5. ______________________ ate peanut butter sandwiches.
6. ______________________ left early.
7. ______________________ don't make good pets.
8. ______________________ found their way home.
9. ______________________ are moving to Denver.

Directions: Write compound predicates to go with these subjects.

10. A scary book ______________________
11. My friend's sister ______________________
12. The shadow ______________________
13. The wind ______________________
14. The runaway car ______________________

 ©2006 Carson-Dellosa Publishing

Name ____________________

Combining Subjects

Too many short sentences make writing sound choppy. Often, we can combine sentences with different subjects and the same predicate to make one sentence with a compound subject.

Example:

Lisa tried out for the play. Todd tried out for the play.
Compound subject: Lisa and Todd tried out for the play.

When sentences have different subjects and different predicates, we cannot combine them this way. Each subject and predicate must stay together. Two short sentences can be combined with a conjunction.

Examples:

Lisa got a part in the play. Todd will help make scenery.
Lisa got a part in the play, and Todd will help make scenery.

Directions: If a pair of sentences share the same predicate, combine them with compound subjects. If the sentences have different subjects and predicates, combine them using **and**.

1. Rachel read a book about explorers. Eric read the same book about explorers.

   ____

2. Rachel really liked the book. Eric agreed with her.

   ____

3. Vicki went to the basketball game last night. Dan went to the basketball game, too.

   ____

4. Vicki lost her coat. Dan missed his ride home.

   ____

5. My uncle planted corn in the garden. My mother planted corn in the garden.

   ____

6. Isaac helped with the food drive last week. Amy helped with the food drive, too.

   ____

©2006 Carson-Dellosa Publishing

Name ______________________

Combining Predicates

If short sentences have the same subject and different predicates, we can combine them into one sentence with a compound predicate.

Example:

Andy got up late this morning.
He nearly missed the school bus.
Compound predicate: Andy got up late this morning and nearly missed the school bus.

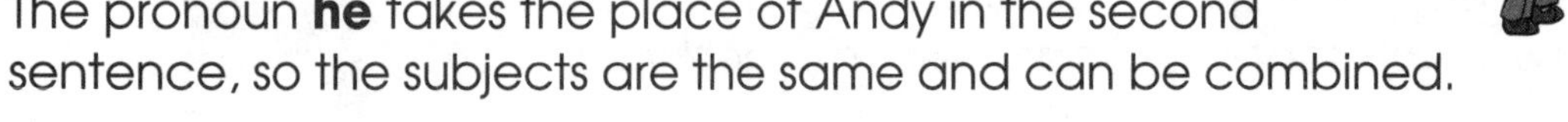

The pronoun **he** takes the place of Andy in the second sentence, so the subjects are the same and can be combined.

When two sentences have different subjects and different predicates, we cannot combine them this way. Two short sentences can be combined with a conjunction.

Examples:

Andy got up late this morning. Cindy woke up early.
Andy got up late this morning, but Cindy woke up early.

Directions: If the pair of sentences share the same subject, combine them with compound predicates. If the sentences have different subjects and predicates, combine them using **and** or **but**.

1. Kyle practiced pitching all winter. Kyle became the pitcher for his team.

   ____

2. Kisha studied two hours for her history test. Angela watched TV.

   ____

3. Jeff had an ear ache. He took medicine four times a day.

   ____

4. Nikki found a new hair style. Melissa didn't like that style.

   ____

5. Kirby buys his lunch every day. Sean brings his lunch from home.

   ____

 ©2006 Carson-Dellosa Publishing

Name ______________________________

Run-On Sentences

A **run-on sentence** occurs when two or more sentences are joined together without the correct punctuation. A run-on sentence must be divided into two or more separate sentences.

Example:

Run-on: On Tuesday my family went to the amusement park but unfortunately it rained and we got wet and it took hours for our clothes to dry.

Correct: On Tuesday, my family went to the amusement park. Unfortunately, it rained and we got wet. It took hours for our clothes to dry.

Directions: Rewrite these run-on sentences correctly.

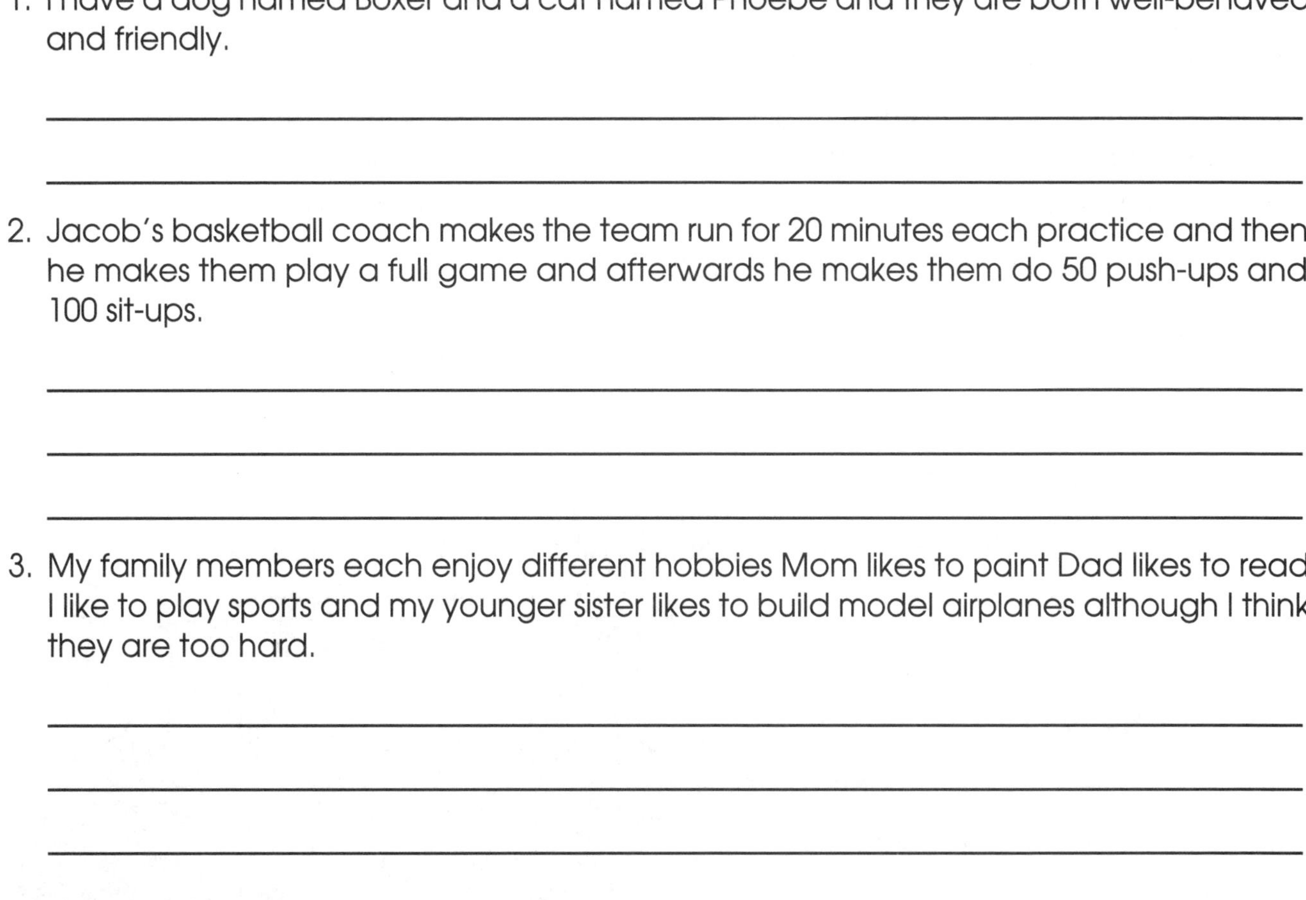

1. I have a dog named Boxer and a cat named Phoebe and they are both well-behaved and friendly.

____

____

2. Jacob's basketball coach makes the team run for 20 minutes each practice and then he makes them play a full game and afterwards he makes them do 50 push-ups and 100 sit-ups.

____

____

____

3. My family members each enjoy different hobbies Mom likes to paint Dad likes to read I like to play sports and my younger sister likes to build model airplanes although I think they are too hard.

____

____

____

____

©2006 Carson-Dellosa Publishing

Name ______________________________

Statements and Questions

A **statement** is a sentence that tells something. It ends with a period (.).

A **question** is a sentence that asks something. It ends with a question mark (?).

Examples:

Statement: Shari is walking to school today.
Question: Is Shari walking to school today?

In some questions, the subject comes between two parts of the verb. In the examples below, the subjects are underlined. The verbs and the rest of the predicates are bold.

Examples:

Is Steve **coming with us**?
Who **will be there**?
Which one did you **select**?

To find the predicate, turn a question into a statement.

Example: Is Steve coming with us? Steve is coming with us.

Directions: Write **S** for statement or **Q** for question. Put a period after the statements and a question mark after the questions.

______ 1. Today is the day for our field trip

______ 2. How are we going to get there

______ 3. The bus will take us

______ 4. Is there room for everyone

______ 5. Who forgot to bring a lunch

______ 6. I'll save you a seat

Directions: Circle the subjects and underline all parts of the predicates.

7. Do you like field trips?
8. Did you bring your coat?
9. Will it be cold there?
10. Do you see my gloves anywhere?
11. Is anyone sitting with you?
12. Does the bus driver have a map?
13. Are all the roads this bumpy?

 ©2006 Carson-Dellosa Publishing

Name ____________________

Commands, Requests and Exclamations

A **command** is a sentence that orders someone to do something. It ends with a period or an exclamation mark (!).

A **request** is a sentence that asks someone to do something. It ends with a period or a question mark (?).

An **exclamation** is a sentence that shows strong feeling. It ends with an exclamation mark (!).

Examples:

Command: Stay in your seat.
Request: Would you please pass the salt?
Please pass the salt.
Exclamation: Call the police!

In the first and last two sentences in the examples, the subject is not stated. The subject is understood to be **you**.

Directions: Write **C** if the sentence is a command, **R** if it is a request and **E** if it is an exclamation. Put the correct punctuation at the end of each sentence.

_______ 1. Look both ways before you cross the street

_______ 2. Please go to the store and buy some bread for us

_______ 3. The house is on fire

_______ 4. Would you hand me the glue

_______ 5. Don't step there

_______ 6. Write your name at the top of the page

_______ 7. Please close the door

_______ 8. Would you answer the phone

_______ 9. Watch out

_______ 10. Take one card from each pile

Name ______________________________

Adjectives

An **adjective** describes a noun or pronoun. There are three types of adjectives. They are **positive**, **comparative** and **superlative**.

Examples:

Positive	**Comparative**	**Superlative**
big	bigger	biggest
beautiful	more beautiful	most beautiful
bright	less bright	least bright

Directions: Write the comparative and superlative forms of these adjectives.

Positive	**Comparative**	**Superlative**
1. happy	____________________	____________________
2. kind	____________________	____________________
3. sad	____________________	____________________
4. slow	____________________	____________________
5. low	____________________	____________________
6. delicious	____________________	____________________
7. strong	____________________	____________________
8. straight	____________________	____________________
9. tall	____________________	____________________
10. humble	____________________	____________________
11. hard	____________________	____________________
12. clear	____________________	____________________
13. loud	____________________	____________________
14. clever	____________________	____________________

 ©2006 Carson-Dellosa Publishing

Name ______________________________

"Good" and "Bad"

When the adjectives **good** and **bad** are used to compare things, the entire word changes.

Examples:

	Comparative	**Superlative**
good	better	best
bad	worse	worst

Use the comparative form of an adjective to compare two people or objects. Use the superlative form to compare three or more people or objects.

Examples:

This is a **good** day.
Tomorrow will be **better** than today.
My birthday is the **best** day of the year.

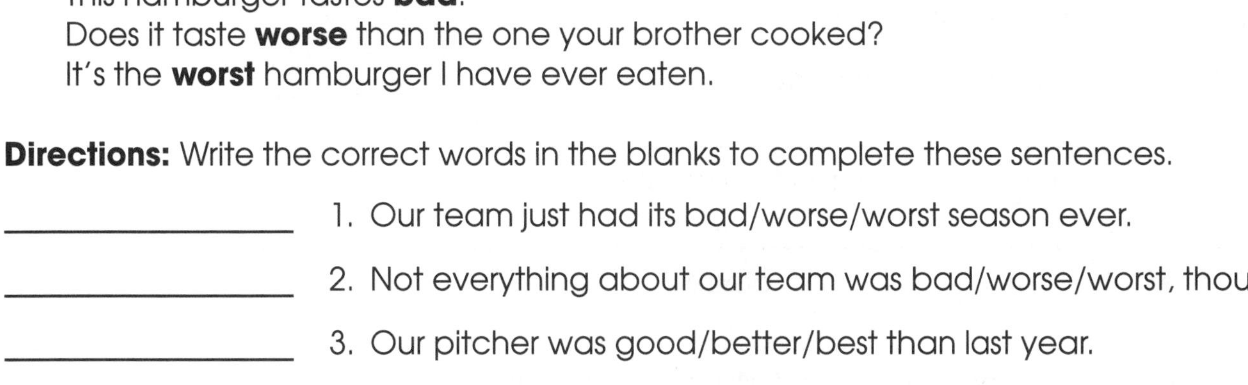

This hamburger tastes **bad**.
Does it taste **worse** than the one your brother cooked?
It's the **worst** hamburger I have ever eaten.

Directions: Write the correct words in the blanks to complete these sentences.

________________ 1. Our team just had its bad/worse/worst season ever.

________________ 2. Not everything about our team was bad/worse/worst, though.

________________ 3. Our pitcher was good/better/best than last year.

________________ 4. Our catcher is the good/better/best in the league.

________________ 5. We had good/better/best uniforms, like we do every year.

________________ 6. I think we just needed good/better/best fielders.

________________ 7. Next season we'll do good/better/best than this one.

________________ 8. We can't do bad/worse/worst than we did this year.

________________ 9. I guess everyone has one bad/worse/worst year.

________________ 10. Now that ours is over, we'll get good/better/best.

©2006 Carson-Dellosa Publishing

Name ______________________________

Adverbs

Adverbs modify verbs. Adverbs tell **when**, **where** or **how**. Many, but not all adverbs, end in **ly**.

Adverbs of time answer the questions **how often** or **when**.

Examples:
The dog escapes its pen **frequently**.
Smart travelers **eventually** will learn to use travelers' checks.

Adverbs of place answer the question **where**.

Example: The police pushed bystanders **away** from the accident scene.

Adverbs of manner answer the questions **how** or **in what manner**.

Example: He **carefully** replaced the delicate vase.

Directions: Underline the verb in each sentence. Circle the adverb. Write the question each adverb answers on the line.

1. My grandmother walks gingerly to avoid falls.

   ____

2. The mice darted everywhere to escape the cat.

   ____

3. He decisively moved the chess piece.

   ____

4. Our family frequently enjoys a night at the movies.

   ____

5. Later, we will discuss the consequences of your behavior.

   ____

6. The audience glanced up at the balcony where the noise originated.

   ____

7. The bleachers are already built for the concert.

   ____

8. My friend and I study daily for the upcoming exams.

   ____

 ©2006 Carson-Dellosa Publishing

Name ______________________

Adverbs

Like adjectives, adverbs have types of comparison. They are positive, comparative and superlative.

Examples:

Positive	**Comparative**	**Superlative**
expertly	more expertly	most expertly
soon	sooner	soonest

Directions: Underline the adverb in each sentence. Then write the degree of comparison on the line.

1. The car easily won the race. ______________
2. Our class most eagerly awaited the return of our test. ______________
3. My ice cream melted more quickly than yours. ______________
4. Frances awoke early the first day of school. ______________
5. He knows well the punishment for disobeying his parents. ______________
6. There is much work to be done on the stadium project. ______________
7. The child played most happily with the building blocks. ______________
8. This article appeared more recently than the other. ______________

Directions: Write the comparative and superlative forms of these adverbs.

Positive	**Comparative**	**Superlative**
9. hard	______________	______________
10. impatiently	______________	______________
11. anxiously	______________	______________
12. suddenly	______________	______________
13. far	______________	______________
14. long	______________	______________

©2006 Carson-Dellosa Publishing

Name ______________________________

Placement of Adjective and Adverb Phrases

Adjectives and adverbs, including prepositional phrases, should be placed as close as possible to the words they describe to avoid confusion.

Example:

Confusing: The boy under the pile of leaves looked for the ball.
(Is the boy or the ball under the pile of leaves?)

Clear: The boy looked under the pile of leaves for the ball.

Directions: Rewrite each sentence by moving the prepositional phrase closer to the word or words it describes. The first one has been done for you.

1. A bird at the pet store bit me in the mall.
   A bird at the pet store in the mall bit me.
2. The woman was looking for her dog in the large hat.
   ____
3. This yard would be great for a dog with a fence.
   ____
4. The car hit the stop sign with the silver stripe.
   ____
5. My cousin with a big bow gave me a present.
   ____
6. The house was near some woods with a pond.
   ____
7. I'll be back to wash the dishes in a minute.
   ____
8. We like to eat eggs in the morning with toast.
   ____
9. He bought a shirt at the new store with short sleeves.
   ____
10. We live in the house down the street with tall windows.
   ____

 ©2006 Carson-Dellosa Publishing

Name ______________________________

Commas

Commas are used to separate items in a series. Both examples below are correct. A final comma is optional.

Examples:

The fruit bowl contains oranges, peaches, pears, and apples.
The fruit bowl contains oranges, peaches, pears and apples.

Commas are also used to separate geographical names and dates.

Examples:

Today's date is January 13, 2000.
My grandfather lives in Tallahassee, Florida.
I would like to visit Paris, France.

Directions: Place commas where needed in these sentences.

1. I was born on September 21 1992.
2. John's favorite sports include basketball football hockey and soccer.
3. The ship will sail on November 16 2004.
4. My family and I vacationed in Salt Lake City Utah.
5. I like to plant beans beets corn and radishes in my garden.
6. Sandy's party will be held in Youngstown Ohio.
7. Periods commas colons and exclamation marks are types of punctuation.
8. Cardinals juncos blue jays finches and sparrows frequent our birdfeeder.
9. My grandfather graduated from high school on June 4 1962.
10. The race will take place in Burlington Vermont.

Directions: Write a sentence using commas to separate words in a series.

11. ______________________________

Directions: Write a sentence using commas to separate geographical names.

12. ______________________________

Directions: Write a sentence using commas to separate dates.

13. ______________________________

Name ______________________

Commas

Commas are used to separate a noun or pronoun in a direct address from the rest of the sentence. A noun or pronoun in a **direct address** is one that names or refers to the person addressed.

Examples:

John, this room is a mess!
This room**, John,** is a disgrace!
Your room needs to be more organized**, John**.

Commas are used to separate an appositive from the rest of the sentence. An **appositive** is a word or words that give the reader more information about a previous noun or pronoun.

Examples:

My teacher, **Ms. Wright**, gave us a test.
Thomas Edison, **the inventor of the lightbulb**, was an interesting man.

Directions: Place commas where needed in these sentences. Then write **appositive** or **direct address** on the line to explain why the commas were used.

1. Melissa do you know the answer? ______________________
2. John the local football hero led the parade through town. ______________________
3. Cancun a Mexican city is a favorite vacation destination. ______________________
4. Please help me move the chair Gail. ______________________
5. My great-grandfather an octogenarian has witnessed many events. ______________________
6. The president of the company Madison Fagan addressed his workers. ______________________
7. My favorite book *Anne of Green Gables* is a joy to read. ______________________
8. Your painting Andre shows great talent. ______________________

 ©2006 Carson-Dellosa Publishing

Name ______________________________

Punctuation

Directions: Add commas where needed. Put the correct punctuation at the end of each sentence.

1. My friend Jamie loves to snowboard
2. Winter sports such as hockey skiing and skating are fun
3. Oh what a lovely view
4. The map shows the continents of Asia Africa Australia and Antarctica
5. My mother a ballet dancer will perform tonight
6. What will you do tomorrow
7. When will the plane arrive at the airport
8. Jason do you know what time it is
9. Friends of ours the Watsons are coming for dinner
10. Margo look out for that falling rock
11. The young child sat reading a book
12. Who wrote this letter
13. My sister Jill is very neat
14. The trampoline is in our backyard
15. We will have chicken peas rice and salad for dinner
16. That dog a Saint Bernard looks dangerous

Name ______________________________

Quotation Marks

When a person's exact words are used in a sentence, **quotation marks** (" ") are used to identify those words. Commas are used to set off the quotation from the rest of the sentence. End punctuation is placed inside the final quotation marks.

Examples:

"When are we leaving?" Joe asked.
Marci shouted, "Go, team!"

When a sentence is interrupted by words that are not part of the quotation (he said, she answered, etc.), they are not included in the quotation marks. Note how commas are used in the next example.

Example: "I am sorry," the man announced, "for my rude behavior."

Directions: Place quotation marks, commas and other punctuation where needed in the sentences below.

1. Watch out yelled Dad.
2. Angela said I don't know how you can eat Brussels sprouts, Ted
3. Put on your coats said Mom. We'll be leaving in 10 minutes
4. Did you hear the assignment asked Joan.
5. Jim shouted This game is driving me up the wall
6. After examining our dog, the veterinarian said He looks healthy and strong
7. The toddlers both wailed We want ice cream
8. The judge announced to the swimmers Take your places
9. Upon receiving the award, the actor said I'd like to thank my friends and family
10. These are my favorite chips said Becky.
11. This test is too hard moaned the class.
12. When their relay team came in first place, the runners shouted, Hooray
13. Where shall we go on vacation this year Dad asked.
14. As we walked past the machinery, the noise was deafening. Cover your ears said Mom.
15. Fire yelled the chef as his pan ignited.
16. I love basketball my little brother stated.

 ©2006 Carson-Dellosa Publishing

Name ______________________________

Capitalization

Directions: Write **C** if capital letters are used correctly or **X** if they are used incorrectly.

_____ 1. Who will win the election for Mayor in November?

_____ 2. Tom Johnson used to be a police officer.

_____ 3. He announced on monday that he wants to be mayor.

_____ 4. My father said he would vote for Tom.

_____ 5. Mom and my sister Judy haven't decided yet.

_____ 6. They will vote at our school.

_____ 7. Every Fall and Spring they put up voting booths there.

_____ 8. I hope the new mayor will do something about our river.

_____ 9. That River is full of chemicals.

_____ 10. I'm glad our water doesn't come from Raven River.

_____ 11. In late Summer, the river actually stinks.

_____ 12. Is every river in our State so dirty?

_____ 13. Scientists check the water every so often.

_____ 14. Some professors from the college even examined it.

_____ 15. That is getting to be a very educated River!

Directions: Write sentences that include:

16. A person's title that should be capitalized.

____

17. The name of a place that should be capitalized.

____

18. The name of a time (day, month, holiday) that should be capitalized.

____

Name ______________________

Combining Sentences

When the subjects are the same, sentences can be combined by using appositives.

Examples:

Tony likes to play basketball. Tony is my neighbor.
Tony, **my neighbor**, likes to play basketball.

Ms. Herman was sick today. Ms. Herman is our math teacher.
Ms. Herman, **our math teacher**, was sick today.

Appositives are set off from the rest of the sentence with commas.

Directions: Use commas and appositives to combine the pairs of sentences.

1. Julie has play practice today. Julie is my sister.

____

2. Greg fixed my bicycle. Greg is my cousin.

____

3. Mr. Scott told us where to meet. Mr. Scott is our coach.

____

4. Tiffany is moving to Detroit. Tiffany is my neighbor.

____

5. Kyle has the flu. Kyle is my brother.

____

6. My favorite football team is playing tonight. Houston is my favorite team.

____

7. Bonnie Pryor will be at our school next week. Bonnie Pryor is a famous author.

____

8. Our neighborhood is having a garage sale. Our neighborhood is the North End.

____

©2006 Carson-Dellosa Publishing

Name ______________________

"Who" Clauses

A **clause** is a group of words with a subject and a verb. When the subject of two sentences is the same person or people, the sentences can sometimes be combined with a "who" clause.

Examples:

Mindy likes animals. Mindy feeds the squirrels.
Mindy, **who likes animals**, feeds the squirrels.

A "who" clause is set off from the rest of the sentence with commas.

Directions: Combine the pairs of sentences, using "who" clauses.

1. Teddy was late to school. Teddy was sorry later.

____

2. Our principal is retiring. Our principal will be 65 this year.

____

3. Michael won the contest. Michael will receive an award.

____

4. Charlene lives next door. Charlene has three cats.

____

5. Burt drew that picture. Burt takes art lessons.

____

6. Marta was elected class president. Marta gave a speech.

____

7. Amy broke her arm. Amy has to wear a cast for 6 weeks.

____

8. Dr. Bank fixed my tooth. He said it would feel better soon.

____

©2006 Carson-Dellosa Publishing

Name ______________________________

"Which" Clauses

When the subject of two sentences is the same thing or things, the sentences can sometimes be combined with a "which" clause.

Examples:

The guppy was first called "the millions fish." The guppy was later named after Reverend Robert Guppy in 1866.
The guppy, **which was first called "the millions fish,"** was later named after Reverend Robert Guppy in 1866.

A "which" clause is set off from the rest of the sentence with commas.

Directions: Combine the pairs of sentences using "which" clauses.

1. Guppies also used to be called rainbow fish. Guppies were brought to Germany in 1908.

____

2. The male guppy is about 1 inch long. The male is smaller than the female.

____

3. The guppies' colors range from red to violet. The colors are brighter in the males.

____

4. Baby guppies hatch from eggs inside the mothers' bodies. The babies are born alive.

____

5. The young are usually born at night. The young are called "fry."

____

6. Female guppies have from 2 to 50 fry at one time. Females sometimes try to eat their fry!

____

7. These fish have been studied by scientists. The fish actually like dirty water.

____

8. Wild guppies eat mosquito eggs. Wild guppies help control the mosquito population.

____

©2006 Carson-Dellosa Publishing

Name ______________________

"That" Clauses

When the subject of two sentences is the same thing or things, the sentences can sometimes be combined with a "that" clause. We use **that** instead of **which** when the clause is very important in the sentence.

Examples:

The store is near our house. The store was closed.
The store **that is near our house** was closed.

The words "**that is near our house**" are very important in the combined sentence. They tell the reader which store was closed. A "that" clause is not set off from the rest of the sentence with commas.

Examples:

Pete's store is near our house. Pete's store was closed.
Pete's store, which is near our house, was closed.

The words "**which is near our house**" are not important to the meaning of the combined sentence. The words **Pete's store** already told us which store was closed.

Directions: Combine the pairs of sentences using "that" clauses.

1. The dog lives next door. The dog chased me.

   ____

2. The bus was taking us to the game. The bus had a flat tire.

   ____

3. The fence is around the school. The fence is painted yellow.

   ____

4. The notebook had my homework in it. The notebook is lost.

   ____

5. A letter came today. The letter was from Mary.

   ____

6. The lamp was fixed yesterday. The lamp doesn't work today.

   ____

7. The lake is by our cabin. The lake is filled with fish.

   ____

Name ______________________________

"That" and "Which" Clauses

Directions: Combine the pairs of sentences using either a "that" or a "which" clause.

1. The TV show was on at 8:00 last night. The TV show was funny.

   ____

2. *The Snappy Show* was on at 8:00 last night. *The Snappy Show* was funny.

   ____

3. The Main Bank is on the corner. The Main Bank is closed today.

   ____

4. The bank is on the corner. The bank is closed today.

   ____

5. The bus takes Dad to work. The bus broke down.

   ____

6. The Broad Street bus takes Dad to work. The Broad Street bus broke down.

   ____

 ©2006 Carson-Dellosa Publishing

Name ______________________________

Combining Sentences

Not every pair of sentences can be combined with "who," "which" or "that" clauses. These sentences can be combined in other ways, either with a conjunction or by renaming the subject.

Examples:

Tim couldn't go to sleep. Todd was sleeping soundly.
Tim couldn't go to sleep, **but** Todd was sleeping soundly.

The zoo keeper fed the baby ape. A crowd gathered to watch.
When the zoo keeper fed the baby ape, a crowd gathered to watch.

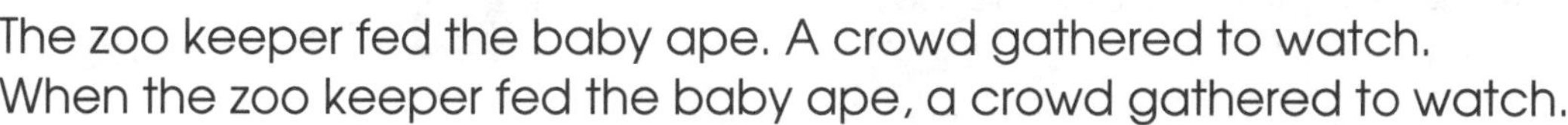

Directions: Combine each pair of sentences using "who," "which" or "that" clauses, by using a conjunction or by renaming the subject.

1. The box slipped off the truck. The box was filled with bottles.

____

2. Carolyn is our scout leader. Carolyn taught us a new game.

____

3. The girl is 8 years old. The girl called the emergency number when her grandmother fell.

____

4. The meatloaf is ready to eat. The salad isn't made yet.

____

5. The rain poured down. The rain canceled our picnic.

____

6. The sixth grade class went on a field trip. The school was much quieter.

____

©2006 Carson-Dellosa Publishing

Name ____________________

"Who's" and "Whose"

Who's is a contraction for **who is.**

Whose is a possessive pronoun.

Examples:
Who's going to come?
Whose shirt is this?

To know which word to use, substitute the words "who is." If the sentence makes sense, use **who's.**

Directions: Write the correct words to complete these sentences.

__________ 1. Do you know who's/whose invited to the party?

__________ 2. I don't even know who's/whose house it will be at.

__________ 3. Who's/Whose towel is on the floor?

__________ 4. Who's/Whose going to drive us?

__________ 5. Who's/Whose ice cream is melting?

__________ 6. I'm the person who's/whose gloves are lost.

__________ 7. Who's/Whose in your group?.

__________ 8. Who's/Whose group is first?

__________ 9. Can you tell who's/whose at the door?

__________ 10. Who's/Whose friend are you?

__________ 11. Who's/Whose cooking tonight?

__________ 12. Who's/Whose cooking do you like best?

 ©2006 Carson-Dellosa Publishing

Name ____________________

"Their," "There" and "They're"

Their is a possessive pronoun meaning "belonging to them."

There is an adverb that indicates place.

They're is a contraction for **they are**.

Examples:

Ron and Sue took **their** dog to the park.
They like to go **there** on Sunday afternoon.
They're probably going back next Sunday, too.

Directions: Write the correct words to complete these sentences.

__________ 1. All the students should bring their/there/they're books to class.

__________ 2. I've never been to France, but I hope to travel their/there/they're someday.

__________ 3. We studied how dolphins care for their/there/they're young.

__________ 4. My parents are going on vacation next week, and their/there/they're taking my sister.

__________ 5. Their/There/They're was a lot of food at the party.

__________ 6. My favorite baseball team lost their/there/they're star pitcher this year.

__________ 7. Those peaches look good, but their/there/they're not ripe yet.

__________ 8. The book is right their/there/they're on the table.

Name ______________________________

"Teach" and "Learn"

Teach is a verb meaning "to explain something." Teach is an irregular verb. Its past tense is **taught**.

Learn is a verb meaning "to gain information."

Examples:

Carrie will **teach** me how to play the piano.
Yesterday she **taught** me "Chopsticks."

I will **learn** a new song every week.
Yesterday I **learned** to play "Chopsticks."

Directions: Write the correct words to complete these sentences.

__________ 1. My brother taught/learned me how to ice skate.

__________ 2. With his help, I taught/learned in three days.

__________ 3. First, I tried to teach/learn skating from a book.

__________ 4. I couldn't teach/learn that way.

__________ 5. You have to try it before you can really teach/learn how to do it.

__________ 6. Now I'm going to teach/learn my cousin.

__________ 7. My cousin already taught/learned how to roller skate.

__________ 8. I shouldn't have any trouble teaching/learning her how to ice skate.

__________ 9. Who taught/learned you how to skate?

__________ 10. My brother taught/learned Mom how to skate, too.

__________ 11. My mother took longer to teach/learn it than I did.

__________ 12. Who will he teach/learn next?

__________ 13. Do you know anyone who wants to teach/learn how to ice skate?

__________ 14. My brother will teach/learn you for free.

__________ 15. You should teach/learn how to ice skate in the wintertime, though. The ice is a little thin in the summer!

©2006 Carson-Dellosa Publishing

Name ______________________________

"Lie" and "Lay"

Lie is a verb meaning "to rest." Lie is an intransitive verb that doesn't need a direct object.

Lay is a verb meaning "to place or put something down." Lay is a transitive verb that requires a direct object.

Examples:

Lie here for a while. (**Lie** has no direct object; **here** is an adverb.)
Lay the book here. (**Lay** has a direct object: **book**.)

Lie and lay are especially tricky because they are both irregular verbs. Notice the past tense of lie is lay!

Present tense	ing form	Past tense	Past participle
lie	lying	lay	has/have/had lain
lay	laying	laid	has/have/had laid

Examples:

I **lie** here today.
I **lay** here yesterday.
I **was lying** there for three hours.

I **lay** the baby in her bed.
I will be **laying** her down in a minute.
I **laid** her in her bed last night, too.

Directions: Write the correct words to complete these sentences.

__________ 1. Shelly lies/lays a blanket on the grass.
__________ 2. Then she lies/lays down in the sun.
__________ 3. Her dog lies/lays there with her.
__________ 4. Yesterday, Shelly lay/laid in the sun for an hour.
__________ 5. The workers are lying/laying bricks for a house.
__________ 6. Yesterday, they lay/laid a ton of them.
__________ 7. They lie/lay one brick on top of the other.
__________ 8. The bricks just lie/lay in a pile until the workers are ready for them.
__________ 9. At lunchtime, some workers lie/lay down for a nap.
__________ 10. Would you like to lie/lay bricks?
__________ 11. Last year, my uncle lay/laid bricks for his new house.
__________ 12. He was so tired every day that he lay/laid down as soon as he finished.

©2006 Carson-Dellosa Publishing

Name ______________________________

"Rise" and "Raise"

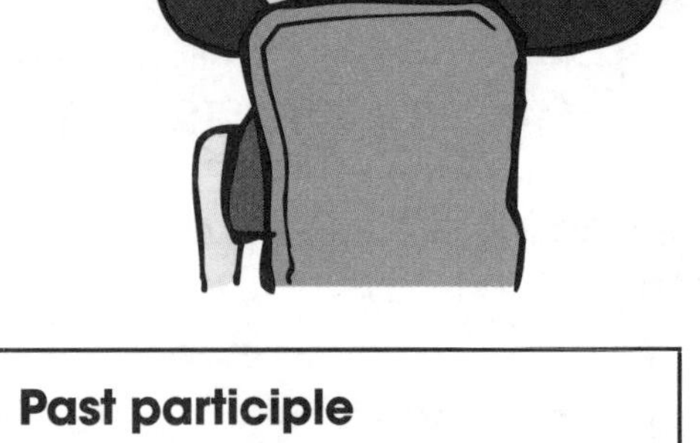

Rise is a verb meaning "to get up" or "to go up." Rise is an intransitive verb that doesn't need a direct object.

Raise is a verb meaning "to lift" or "to grow." Raise is a transitive verb that requires a direct object.

Examples:

The curtain **rises**.
The girl **raises** her hand.

Raise is a regular verb. Rise is irregular.

Present tense	Past tense	Past participle
rise	rose	has/have/had risen
raise	raised	has/have/had raised

Examples:

The sun **rose** this morning.
The boy **raised** the window higher.

Directions: Write the correct words to complete these sentences.

__________ 1. This bread dough rises/raises in an hour.
__________ 2. The landlord will rise/raise the rent.
__________ 3. The balloon rose/raised into the sky.
__________ 4. My sister rose/raised the seat on my bike.
__________ 5. The baby rose/raised the spoon to his mouth.
__________ 6. The eagle rose/raised out of sight.
__________ 7. The farmer rises/raises pigs.
__________ 8. The scouts rose/raised the flag.
__________ 9. When the fog rose/raised, we could see better.
__________ 10. The price of ice cream rose/raised again.
__________ 11. The king rose/raised the glass to his lips.
__________ 12. Rise/Raise the picture on that wall higher.

 ©2006 Carson-Dellosa Publishing

Name ____________________

"All Right," "All Ready" and "Already"

All right means "well enough" or "very well." Sometimes **all right** is incorrectly spelled. **Alright** is not a word.

Example:

Correct: We'll be all right when the rain stops.
Incorrect: Are you feeling **alright** today?

All ready is an adjective meaning "completely ready."

Already is an adverb meaning "before this time" or "by this time."

Examples:

Are you **all ready** to go?
He was **already** there when I arrived.

Directions: Write the correct words to complete these sentences.

__________ 1. The children are all ready/already for the picnic.

__________ 2. Ted was all ready/already late for the show.

__________ 3. Is your sister going to be all right/alright?

__________ 4. I was all ready/already tired before the race began.

__________ 5. Joan has all ready/already left for the dance.

__________ 6. Will you be all right/alright by yourself?

__________ 7. We are all ready/already for our talent show.

__________ 8. I all ready/already read that book.

__________ 9. I want to be all ready/already when they get here.

__________ 10. Dad was sick, but he's all right/alright now.

__________ 11. The dinner is all ready/already to eat.

__________ 12. Cathy all ready/already wrote her report.

©2006 Carson-Dellosa Publishing

Name ____________________

"Accept" and "Except"/"Affect" and "Effect"

Accept is a verb meaning "to receive."

Except can be used as a verb or a preposition. As a verb, it means "to leave out." As a preposition, it means "excluding."

Examples:

I will **accept** the invitation to the dinner dance.
No one **except** Robert will receive an award.

Affect is a verb meaning "to impress one's thoughts or feelings."

Effect can be used as a noun or a verb. As a verb, it means "to accomplish." As a noun, it means "the result of an action."

Examples:

Her attitude may **affect** her performance on the test.
He **effected** several changes during his first few months as governor.
The **effects** of the storm will be felt for some time.

Directions: Write the correct words to complete these sentences.

__________ 1. My partner and I will work to affect/effect attitudes toward rainforest renewal.
__________ 2. He courageously accepted/excepted the challenge of a chess duel.
__________ 3. The affect/effect of the strike by truck drivers was felt nationwide.
__________ 4. The new CEO of the company sought to affect/effect a change in company morale.
__________ 5. Everyone accept/except Marlene will attend the game.
__________ 6. My grandmother will never accept/except the fact that she can no longer drive.
__________ 7. Accept/Except for this chewing incident, my puppy has been well-behaved.
__________ 8. The sights of the war affected/effected soldiers for the rest of their lives.
__________ 9. What affect/effect will the drop in the stock market have on the average person?
__________ 10. The affect/effect of the wind was devastating.
__________ 11. How will cheating on a test affect/effect your reputation?
__________ 12. I would like to go to the park on any day accept/except Monday.

 ©2006 Carson-Dellosa Publishing

Name ______________________________

Synonyms

Synonyms are words that mean the same or nearly the same.

Examples:
- **small** and **little**
- **big** and **large**
- **bright** and **shiny**
- **unhappy** and **sad**

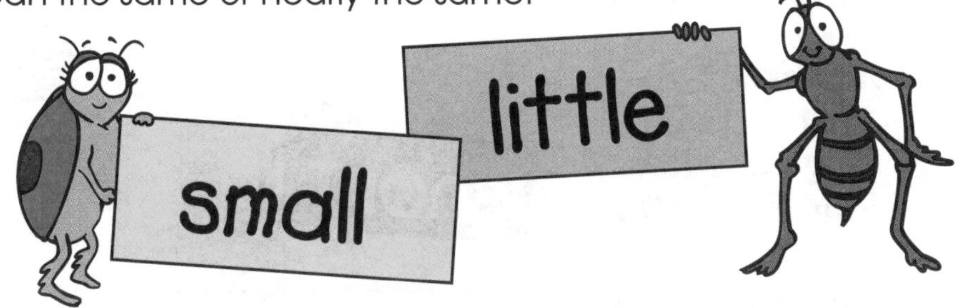

Directions: Write a synonym for each word. Then use it in a sentence. Use a dictionary if you are unsure of the meaning of a word.

1. cup ______________________________
____
2. book ______________________________
____
3. looking glass ______________________________
____
4. hop ______________________________
____
5. discover ______________________________
____
6. plan ______________________________
____
7. lamp ______________________________
____
8. friend ______________________________
____
9. discuss ______________________________
____
10. rotate ______________________________
____

Name ____________________

Antonyms

Antonyms are words that mean the opposite.

Examples:
tall and **short**
high and **low**
top and **bottom**

Directions: Write an antonym for each word. Then use it in a sentence. Use a dictionary if you are unsure of the meaning of a word.

1. tired ____________________
____
2. bright ____________________
____
3. sparkling ____________________
____
4. tame ____________________
____
5. fresh ____________________
____
6. elegant ____________________
____
7. real ____________________
____
8. odd ____________________
____
9. unruly ____________________
____
10. valor ____________________
____

 ©2006 Carson-Dellosa Publishing

Name ______________________

Homophones

Homophones are words that are pronounced the same but are spelled differently and have different meanings.

Example: to, two, too

Directions: Write sentences using these homophones. Use a dictionary if you are unsure of the meaning of a word.

1. would ______________________
2. wood ______________________
3. sight ______________________
4. site ______________________
5. principal ______________________
6. principle ______________________
7. stationary ______________________
8. stationery ______________________
9. pain ______________________
10. pane ______________________
11. fur ______________________
12. fir ______________________
13. kernel ______________________
14. colonel ______________________
15. serial ______________________
16. cereal ______________________

©2006 Carson-Dellosa Publishing

Name ______________________________

Similes

A **simile** uses the words **like** or **as** to compare two things.

Examples:

The snow glittered **like** diamonds.
He was **as** slow **as** a turtle.

Directions: Circle the two objects being compared in each sentence.

1. The kittens were like gymnasts performing tricks.
2. My old computer is as slow as molasses.
3. When the lights went out in the basement, it was as dark as night.
4. The sun was like a fire, heating up the earth.
5. The young girl was as graceful as a ballerina.
6. The puppy cried like a baby all night.
7. He flies that airplane like a daredevil.
8. The girl was as pretty as a picture.
9. The snow on the mountain tops was like whipped cream.
10. The tiger's eyes were like emeralds.

Directions: Complete the simile in each sentence.

11. My cat is as ______________________ as ______________________.
12. He was as ______________________ as ______________________.
13. Melissa's eyes shone like ______________________.
14. The paints were like ______________________.
15. The opera singer's voice was as ______________ as ______________.

 ©2006 Carson-Dellosa Publishing

Name ______________________________

Metaphors

A **metaphor** makes a direct comparison between two unlike things. A noun must be used in the comparison. The words **like** and **as** are not used.

Examples:

Correct: The exuberant puppy was a **bundle of energy**.
Incorrect: The dog is **happy**. (**Happy** is an adjective.)

Directions: Circle the two objects being compared.

1. The old truck was a heap of rusty metal.
2. The moon was a silver dollar in the sky.
3. Their vacation was a nightmare.
4. That wasp is a flying menace.
5. The prairie was a carpet of green.
6. The flowers were jewels on stems.
7. This winter, our pond is glass.

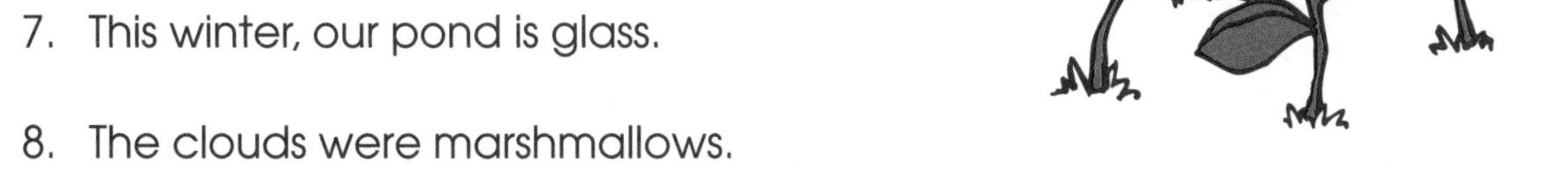

8. The clouds were marshmallows.

Directions: Complete the metaphor in each sentence.

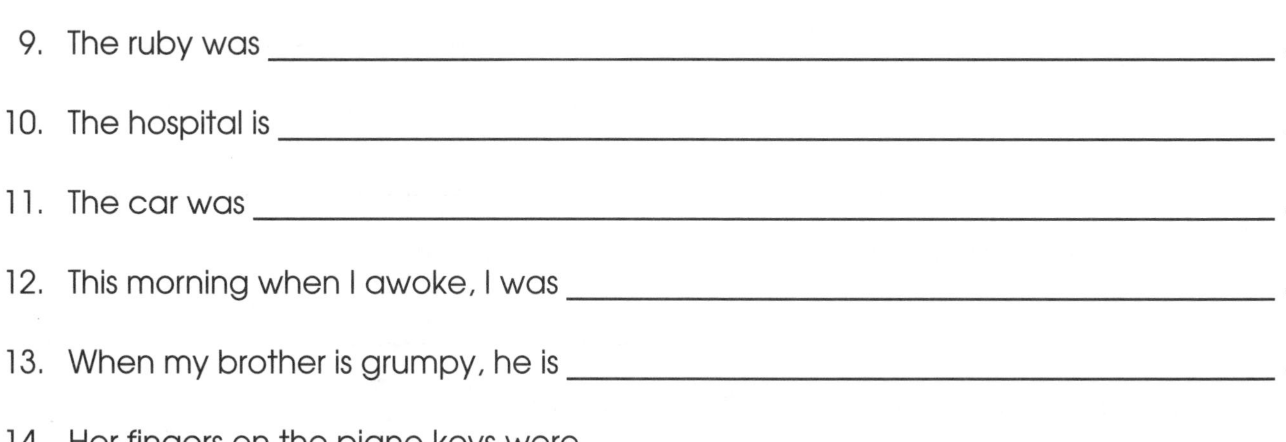

9. The ruby was ______________________________.
10. The hospital is ______________________________.
11. The car was ______________________________.
12. This morning when I awoke, I was ______________________________.
13. When my brother is grumpy, he is ______________________________.
14. Her fingers on the piano keys were ______________________________.

Name ______________________________

Idioms

An **idiom** is a phrase that says one thing but actually means something quite different.

Example: Raining cats and dogs means it is raining very hard.

Directions: Underline the idiom in each sentence. Write its meaning on the line.

1. She won the race by the skin of her teeth.

   ____

2. The opera singer was a bundle of nerves before her performance.

   ____

3. Before the audition began, the girl's mother told her to break a leg.

   ____

4. I'll be a basket case before this test is over.

   ____

5. There is a lot of red tape in order to get a marriage license.

   ____

6. My friend and I decided to bury the hatchet after our fight.

   ____

7. He is so oblivious, he might as well have his head in the sand.

   ____

8. He was at the end of his rope after losing his job.

   ____

 ©2006 Carson-Dellosa Publishing

Name ____________________

Descriptive Sentences

Descriptive sentences give readers a vivid image and enable them to imagine a scene clearly.

Example:

Nondescriptive sentence: There were grapes in the bowl.
Descriptive sentence: The plump purple grapes in the bowl looked tantalizing.

Directions: Rewrite these sentences using descriptive language.

1. The dog walked in its pen.

____

2. The turkey was almost done.

____

3. I became upset when my computer wouldn't work.

____

4. Jared and Michelle went to the ice-cream parlor.

____

5. The telephone kept ringing.

____

6. I wrote a story.

____

7. The movie was excellent.

____

8. Dominique was upset that her friend was ill.

____

©2006 Carson-Dellosa Publishing

Name ______________________________

Writing Fiction

Directions: Use descriptive writing to complete each story. Write at least five sentences.

1. It was a cold, wintry morning in January. Snow had fallen steadily for 4 days. I was staring out my bedroom window when I saw the bedraggled dog staggering through the snow.

____
____
____
____
____
____

2. Mindy was home Saturday studying for a big science test. Report cards were due next Friday, and the test on Monday would be on the report card. Mindy needed to do well on the test to get an A in Science. The phone rang. It was her best friend, Jenny.

____
____
____
____
____
____

3. Martin works every weekend delivering newspapers. He wakes up at 5:30 A.M. and begins his route at 6:00 A.M. He delivers 150 newspapers on his bike. He enjoys his weekend job because he is working toward a goal.

____
____
____
____
____
____

 ©2006 Carson-Dellosa Publishing

Name ______________________

Newspaper Articles

In a newspaper article, the most important facts of the story are included in the first sentence or two. This includes answers to the questions **who**, **what**, **when**, **where**, **why** and **how**? The details are filled in later in the article.

Directions: Attach a copy of a newspaper article to this page. Read the article, then answer these questions.

1. **What** happened? ______________________
2. **When** did it happen? ______________________
3. **Who** did it happen to? ______________________
4. **Where** did it happen? ______________________
5. **How** did it happen? ______________________
6. **Why** did it happen? ______________________
7. Reporters try to add an eye-catching headline so people will want to read the article. What was the headline of the newspaper article you read?

   ____

Directions: Write a newspaper article about a real or fictional event.

8. ______________________

   ____

   ____

   ____

   ____

   ____

©2006 Carson-Dellosa Publishing

Name ______________________

Friendly Letters

A **friendly letter** has these parts: return address, date, greeting, body, closing and signature.

Directions: Read this letter. Then label the parts of the letter.

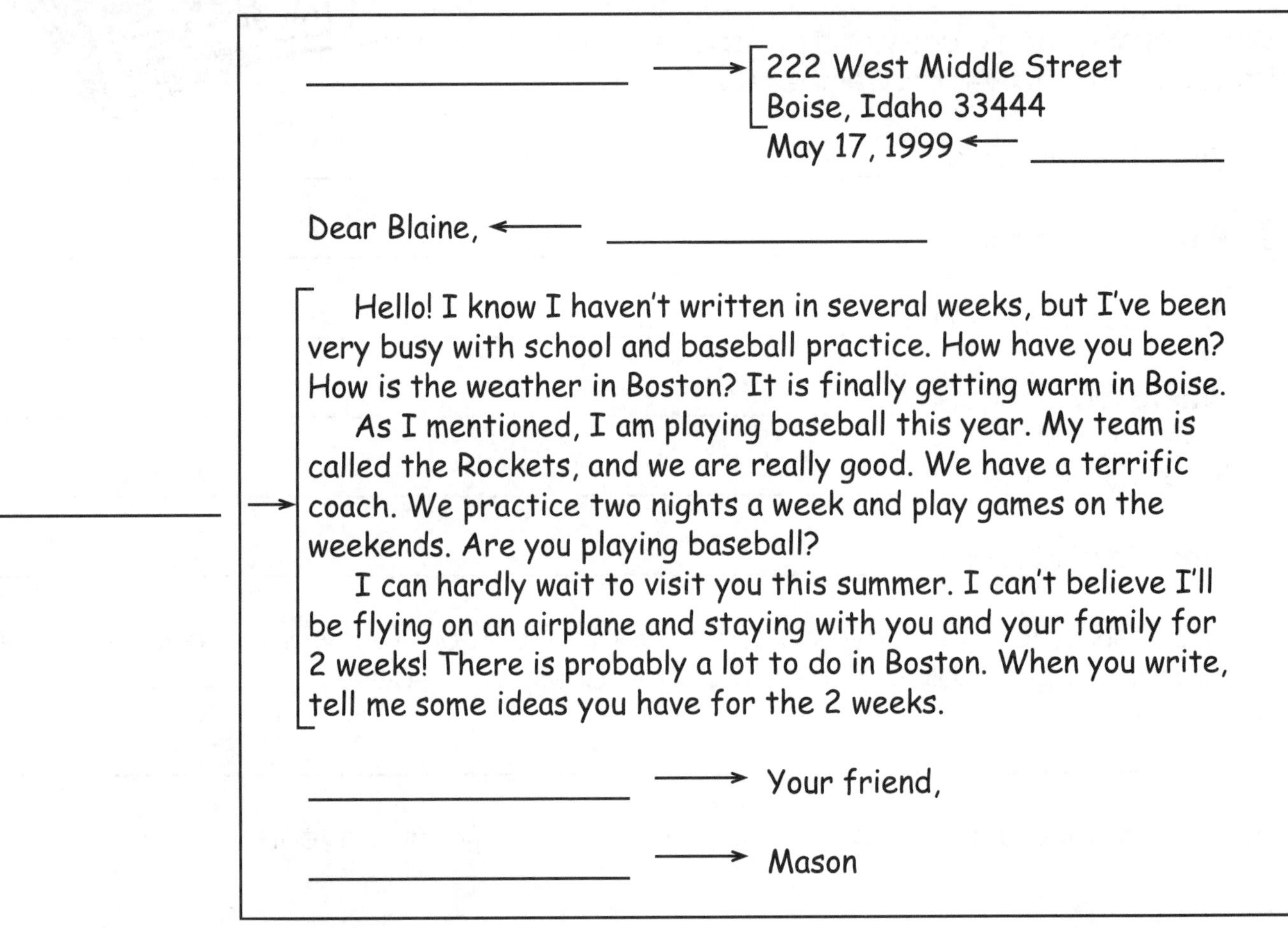

______________ → 222 West Middle Street
Boise, Idaho 33444
May 17, 1999 ← ______________

Dear Blaine, ← ______________

______________ →

Hello! I know I haven't written in several weeks, but I've been very busy with school and baseball practice. How have you been? How is the weather in Boston? It is finally getting warm in Boise.

As I mentioned, I am playing baseball this year. My team is called the Rockets, and we are really good. We have a terrific coach. We practice two nights a week and play games on the weekends. Are you playing baseball?

I can hardly wait to visit you this summer. I can't believe I'll be flying on an airplane and staying with you and your family for 2 weeks! There is probably a lot to do in Boston. When you write, tell me some ideas you have for the 2 weeks.

______________ → Your friend,

______________ → Mason

Envelopes should follow this format:

Mason Fitch
222 West Middle Street
Boise, ID 33444

Blaine Morgan
111 E. 9th Street, Apt 22B
Boston, MA 00011

 ©2006 Carson-Dellosa Publishing

Name ______________________________

Friendly Letters

Directions: Write a friendly letter. Then address the envelope.

Name ______________________

Invitations

An **invitation** must include the time, date and place of the event or party. It is also helpful to include the reason for the event, such as a birthday, anniversary, etc.

If the sender wants to know how many people will attend the event, he or she adds RSVP. **RSVP** means the receiver should let the sender know whether or not he/she will attend.

Example:

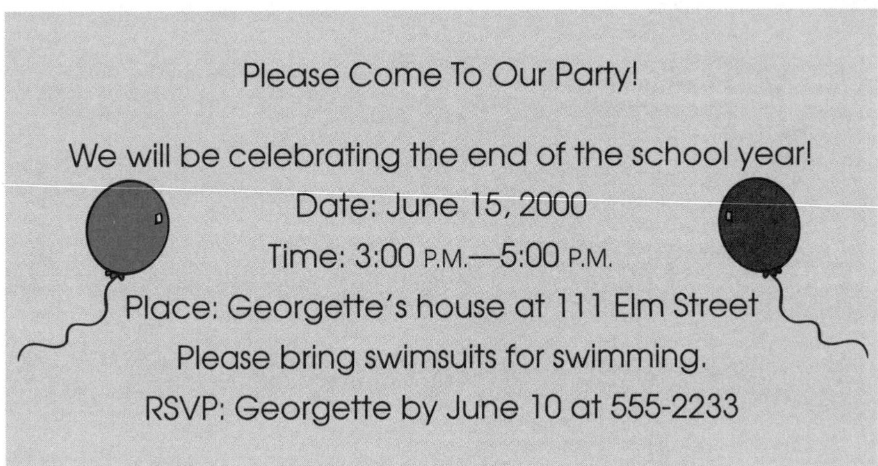
Please Come To Our Party!

We will be celebrating the end of the school year!

Date: June 15, 2000

Time: 3:00 P.M.—5:00 P.M.

Place: Georgette's house at 111 Elm Street

Please bring swimsuits for swimming.

RSVP: Georgette by June 10 at 555-2233

Directions: Write an invitation to a real or imaginary event. Include all relevant information.

 ©2006 Carson-Dellosa Publishing

Name ______________________________

Thank You Notes

A **thank you note** should be written and sent when a gift is received or when someone does something particularly nice. For example, if you spent the day with a friend's parents at their cottage, you should write a thank you note.

Even though your note may be informal, it is important to follow the correct format, which includes the date, an appropriate closing and your signature.

Example:

January 19, 1999

Dear Setsuko,

Thank you very much for your latest letter and pictures. Since we became pen pals, I have learned so much about Japan and your culture. Your mother's garden is beautiful. I wish we had flowers in America like the ones in the pictures. I will be sending a longer letter soon.

Your friend,

Lakeesha

Directions: Write a thank you note.

____

____

____

____

____

____

©2006 Carson-Dellosa Publishing

Name ______________________________

Haiku

Haiku is a form of unrhymed Japanese poetry. Haiku have three lines. The first line has five syllables, the second line has seven syllables and the third line has five syllables.

Example:

The Fall

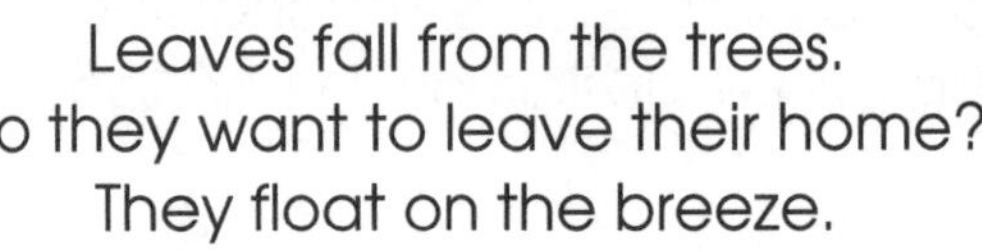

Leaves fall from the trees.
Do they want to leave their home?
They float on the breeze.

Directions: Write a haiku about nature. Write the title on the first line. Then illustrate your haiku.

Nature ______________________________

____

____

____

 ©2006 Carson-Dellosa Publishing

Name ___________________________

Lantern

Lantern is another type of five-line Japanese poetry. It takes the shape of a Japanese lantern. Each line must contain the following number of syllables.

Line 1: 1 syllable
Line 2: 2 syllables
Line 3: 3 syllables
Line 4: 4 syllables
Line 5: 1 syllable

Example:

Cats—
Stealthy
wild creatures
want to be your
pet.

Directions: Write and illustrate your own lantern.

____

____

____

____

____

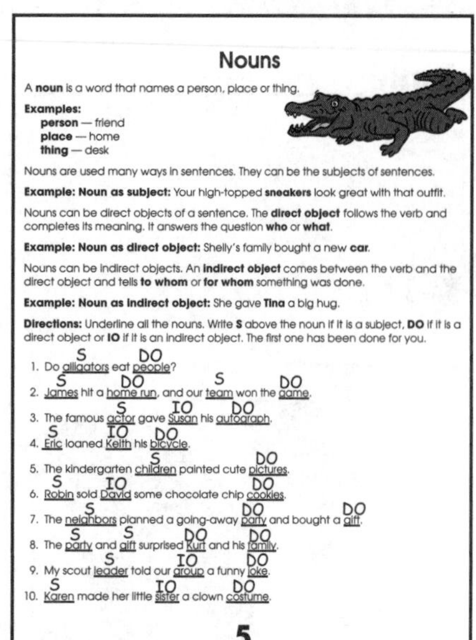

Nouns

A **noun** is a word that names a person, place or thing.

Examples:
person — friend
place — home
thing — desk

Nouns are used many ways in sentences. They can be the subjects of sentences.

Example: Noun as subject: Your high-topped **sneakers** look great with that outfit.

Nouns can be direct objects of a sentence. The **direct object** follows the verb and completes its meaning. It answers the question **who** or **what**.

Example: Noun as direct object: Shelly's family bought a new **car**.

Nouns can be indirect objects. An **indirect object** comes between the verb and the direct object and tells **to whom** or **for whom** something was done.

Example: Noun as indirect object: She gave **Tina** a big hug.

Directions: Underline all the nouns. Write **S** above the noun if it is a subject, **DO** if it is a direct object or **IO** if it is an indirect object. The first one has been done for you.

1. Do alligators (S) eat people (DO)?
2. James (S) hit a home run (DO), and our team (S) won the game (DO).
3. The famous actor (S) gave Susan (IO) his autograph (DO).
4. Eric (S) loaned Keith (IO) his bicycle (DO).
5. The kindergarten children (S) painted cute pictures (DO).
6. Robin (S) sold David (IO) some chocolate chip cookies (DO).
7. The neighbors (S) planned a going-away party (DO) and bought a gift (DO).
8. The party (S) and gift (S) surprised Kurt (DO) and his family (DO).
9. My scout leader (S) told our group (IO) a funny joke (DO).
10. Karen (S) made her little sister (IO) a clown costume (DO).

5

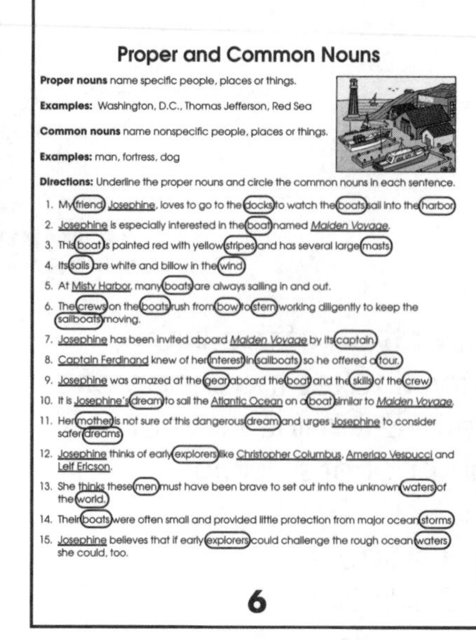

Proper and Common Nouns

Proper nouns name specific people, places or things.

Examples: Washington, D.C., Thomas Jefferson, Red Sea

Common nouns name nonspecific people, places or things.

Examples: man, fortress, dog

Directions: Underline the proper nouns and circle the common nouns in each sentence.

1. My friend Josephine, loves to go to the docks to watch the boats sail into the harbor.
2. Josephine is especially interested in the boat named *Maiden Voyage*.
3. This boat is painted red with yellow stripes and has several large masts.
4. Its sails are white and billow in the wind.
5. At Misty Harbor, many boats are always sailing in and out.
6. The crews on the boats rush from bow to stern working diligently to keep the sailboats moving.
7. Josephine has been invited aboard *Maiden Voyage* by its captain.
8. Captain Ferdinand knew of her interest in sailboats so he offered a tour.
9. Josephine was amazed at the gear aboard the boat and the skills of the crew.
10. It is Josephine's dream to sail the Atlantic Ocean on a boat similar to *Maiden Voyage*.
11. Her mother is not sure of this dangerous dream and urges Josephine to consider safer dreams.
12. Josephine thinks of early explorers like Christopher Columbus, Amerigo Vespucci and Leif Ericson.
13. She thinks these men must have been brave to set out into the unknown waters of the world.
14. Their boats were often small and provided little protection from major ocean storms.
15. Josephine believes that if early explorers could challenge the rough ocean waters she could, too.

6

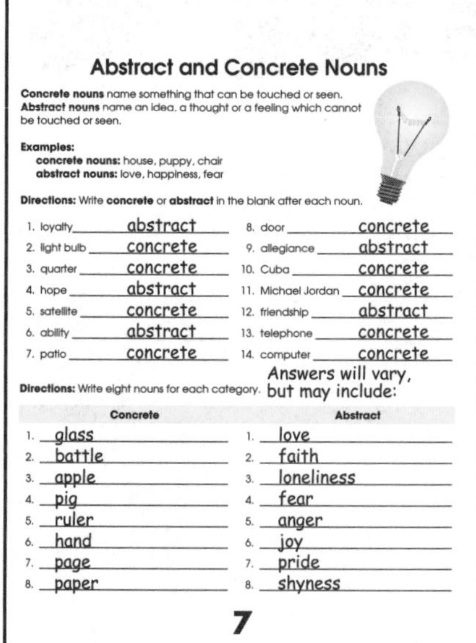

Abstract and Concrete Nouns

Concrete nouns name something that can be touched or seen.
Abstract nouns name an idea, a thought or a feeling which cannot be touched or seen.

Examples:
concrete nouns: house, puppy, chair
abstract nouns: love, happiness, fear

Directions: Write **concrete** or **abstract** in the blank after each noun.

1. loyalty abstract
2. light bulb concrete
3. quarter concrete
4. hope abstract
5. satellite concrete
6. ability abstract
7. patio concrete
8. door concrete
9. allegiance abstract
10. Cuba concrete
11. Michael Jordan concrete
12. friendship abstract
13. telephone concrete
14. computer concrete

Directions: Write eight nouns for each category. Answers will vary, but may include:

	Concrete		Abstract
1.	glass	1.	love
2.	battle	2.	faith
3.	apple	3.	loneliness
4.	pig	4.	fear
5.	ruler	5.	anger
6.	hand	6.	joy
7.	page	7.	pride
8.	paper	8.	shyness

7

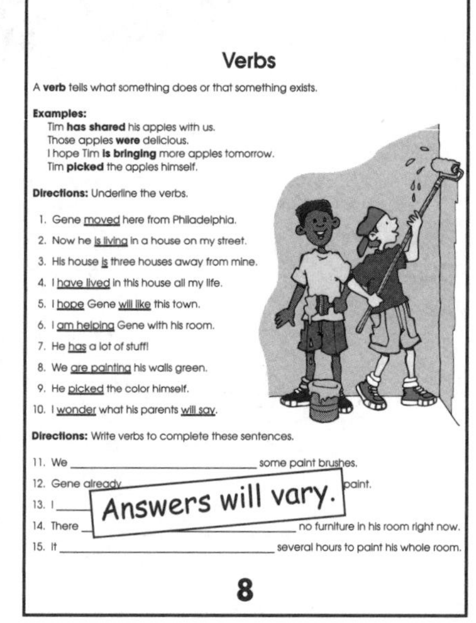

Verbs

A **verb** tells what something does or that something exists.

Examples:
Tim **has shared** his apples with us.
Those apples **were** delicious.
I hope Tim **is bringing** more apples tomorrow.
Tim **picked** the apples himself.

Directions: Underline the verbs.

1. Gene moved here from Philadelphia.
2. Now he is living in a house on my street.
3. His house is three houses away from mine.
4. I have lived in this house all my life.
5. I hope Gene will like this town.
6. I am helping Gene with his room.
7. He has a lot of stuff!
8. We are painting his walls green.
9. He picked the color himself.
10. I wonder what his parents will say.

Directions: Write verbs to complete these sentences.

11. We ________ some paint brushes.
12. Gene already ________ paint.
13. I ________
14. There ________ no furniture in his room right now.
15. It ________ several hours to paint his whole room.

Answers will vary.

8

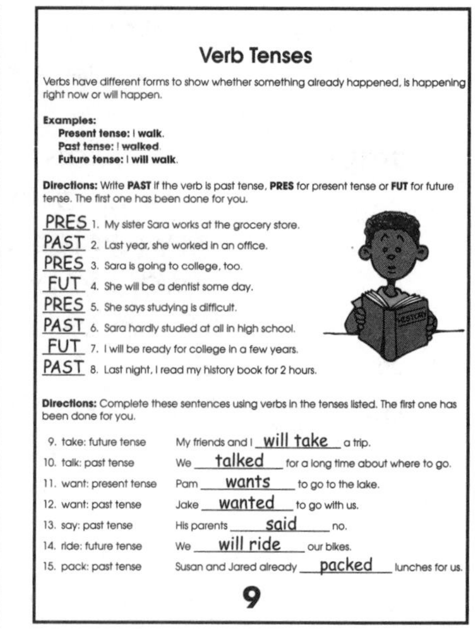

Verb Tenses

Verbs have different forms to show whether something already happened, is happening right now or will happen.

Examples:
Present tense: I walk.
Past tense: I walked.
Future tense: I will walk.

Directions: Write **PAST** if the verb is past tense, **PRES** for present tense or **FUT** for future tense. The first one has been done for you.

PRES 1. My sister Sara works at the grocery store.
PAST 2. Last year, she worked in an office.
PRES 3. Sara is going to college, too.
FUT 4. She will be a dentist some day.
PRES 5. She says studying is difficult.
PAST 6. Sara hardly studied at all in high school.
FUT 7. I will be ready for college in a few years.
PAST 8. Last night, I read my history book for 2 hours.

Directions: Complete these sentences using verbs in the tenses listed. The first one has been done for you.

9. take: future tense — My friends and I will take a trip.
10. talk: past tense — We talked for a long time about where to go.
11. want: present tense — Pam wants to go to the lake.
12. want: past tense — Jake wanted to go with us.
13. say: past tense — His parents said no.
14. ride: future tense — We will ride our bikes.
15. pack: past tense — Susan and Jared already packed lunches for us.

9

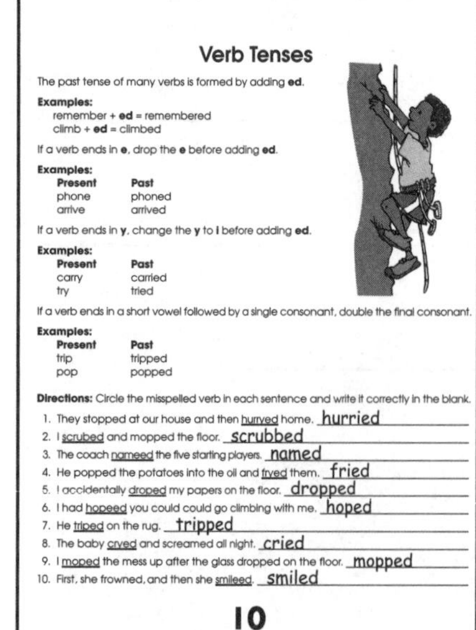

Verb Tenses

The past tense of many verbs is formed by adding **ed**.

Examples:
remember + **ed** = remembered
climb + **ed** = climbed

If a verb ends in **e**, drop the **e** before adding **ed**.

Examples:

Present	Past
phone	phoned
arrive	arrived

If a verb ends in **y**, change the **y** to **i** before adding **ed**.

Examples:

Present	Past
carry	carried
try	tried

If a verb ends in a short vowel followed by a single consonant, double the final consonant.

Examples:

Present	Past
trip	tripped
pop	popped

Directions: Circle the misspelled verb in each sentence and write it correctly in the blank.

1. They stopped at our house and then hurryed home. hurried
2. I scrubed and mopped the floor. scrubbed
3. The coach nameed the five starting players. named
4. He popped the potatoes into the oil and fryed them. fried
5. I accidentally droped my papers on the floor. dropped
6. I had hopeed you could could go climbing with me. hoped
7. He triped on the rug. tripped
8. The baby cryed and screamed all night. cried
9. I moped the mess up after the glass dropped on the floor. mopped
10. First, she frowned, and then she smileed. smiled

10

Principal Parts of Verbs

Verbs have three principal parts. They are **present**, **past** and **past participle**.

Regular verbs form the past tense by adding **ed** to the present tense.

The past participle is formed by using the past tense verb with a helping verb: **has**, **have** or **had**.

Directions: Write the correct form of each verb. The first one has been done for you.

Present	Past	Past Participle
1. look	looked	has/have/had looked
2. plan	planned	has/have/had planned
3. close	closed	has/have/had closed
4. wash	washed	has/have/had washed
5. prepare	prepared	has/have/had prepared
6. provide	provided	has/have/had provided
7. invite	invited	has/have/had invited
8. discover	discovered	has/have/had discovered
9. approve	approved	has/have/had approved
10. search	searched	has/have/had searched
11. establish	established	has/have/had established
12. form	formed	has/have/had formed
13. push	pushed	has/have/had pushed
14. travel	traveled	has/have/had traveled

11

©2006 Carson-Dellosa Publishing

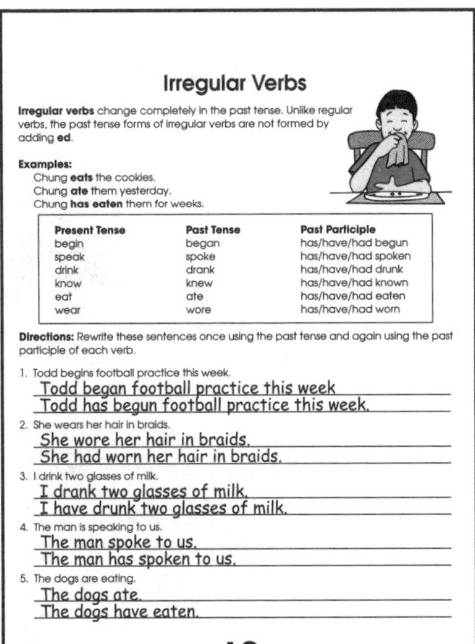

Irregular Verbs

Irregular verbs change completely in the past tense. Unlike regular verbs, the past tense forms of irregular verbs are not formed by adding **ed**.

Examples:
Chung **eats** the cookies.
Chung **ate** them yesterday.
Chung **has eaten** them for weeks.

Present Tense	Past Tense	Past Participle
begin	began	has/have/had begun
speak	spoke	has/have/had spoken
drink	drank	has/have/had drunk
know	knew	has/have/had known
eat	ate	has/have/had eaten
wear	wore	has/have/had worn

Directions: Rewrite these sentences once using the past tense and again using the past participle of each verb.

1. Todd begins football practice this week.
Todd began football practice this week
Todd has begun football practice this week.
2. She wears her hair in braids.
She wore her hair in braids.
She had worn her hair in braids.
3. I drink two glasses of milk.
I drank two glasses of milk.
I have drunk two glasses of milk.
4. The man is speaking to us.
The man spoke to us.
The man has spoken to us.
5. The dogs are eating.
The dogs ate.
The dogs have eaten.

12

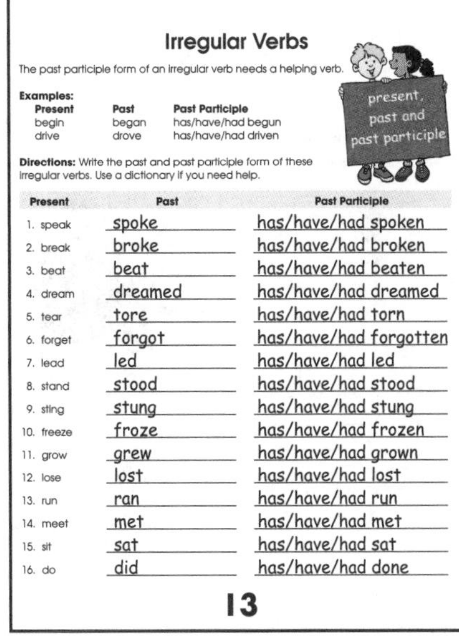

Irregular Verbs

The past participle form of an irregular verb needs a helping verb.

Examples:

Present	Past	Past Participle
begin	began	has/have/had begun
drive	drove	has/have/had driven

Directions: Write the past and past participle form of these irregular verbs. Use a dictionary if you need help.

Present	Past	Past Participle
1. speak	spoke	has/have/had spoken
2. break	broke	has/have/had broken
3. beat	beat	has/have/had beaten
4. dream	dreamed	has/have/had dreamed
5. tear	tore	has/have/had torn
6. forget	forgot	has/have/had forgotten
7. lead	led	has/have/had led
8. stand	stood	has/have/had stood
9. sting	stung	has/have/had stung
10. freeze	froze	has/have/had frozen
11. grow	grew	has/have/had grown
12. lose	lost	has/have/had lost
13. run	ran	has/have/had run
14. meet	met	has/have/had met
15. sit	sat	has/have/had sat
16. do	did	has/have/had done

13

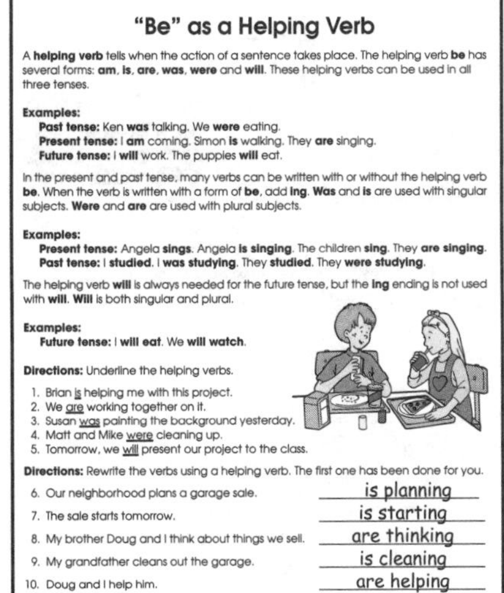

"Be" as a Helping Verb

A **helping verb** tells when the action of a sentence takes place. The helping verb **be** has several forms: **am**, **is**, **are**, **was**, **were** and **will**. These helping verbs can be used in all three tenses.

Examples:
Past tense: Ken **was** talking. We **were** eating.
Present tense: I **am** coming. Simon **is** walking. They **are** singing.
Future tense: I **will** work. The puppies **will** eat.

In the present and past tense, many verbs can be written with or without the helping verb **be**. When the verb is written with a form of **be**, add **ing**. **Was** and **is** are used with singular subjects. **Were** and **are** are used with plural subjects.

Examples:
Present tense: Angela **sings**. Angela **is singing**. The children **sing**. They **are singing**.
Past tense: I **studied**. I **was studying**. They **studied**. They **were studying**.

The helping verb **will** is always needed for the future tense, but the **ing** ending is not used with **will**. **Will** is both singular and plural.

Examples:
Future tense: I **will eat**. We **will watch**.

Directions: Underline the helping verbs.

1. Brian is helping me with this project.
2. We are working together on it.
3. Susan was painting the background yesterday.
4. Matt and Mike were cleaning up.
5. Tomorrow, we will present our project to the class.

Directions: Rewrite the verbs using a helping verb. The first one has been done for you.

6. Our neighborhood plans a garage sale. is planning
7. The sale starts tomorrow. is starting
8. My brother Doug and I think about things we sell. are thinking
9. My grandfather cleans out the garage. is cleaning
10. Doug and I help him. are helping

14

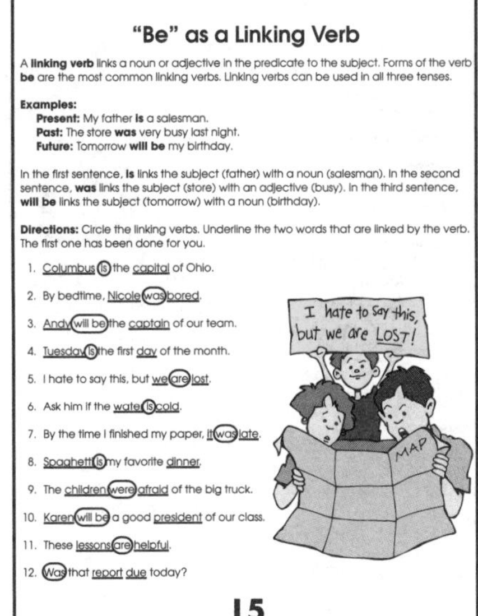

"Be" as a Linking Verb

A **linking verb** links a noun or adjective in the predicate to the subject. Forms of the verb **be** are the most common linking verbs. Linking verbs can be used in all three tenses.

Examples:
Present: My father **is** a salesman.
Past: The store **was** very busy last night.
Future: Tomorrow **will be** my birthday.

In the first sentence, **is** links the subject (father) with a noun (salesman). In the second sentence, **was** links the subject (store) with an adjective (busy). In the third sentence, **will be** links the subject (tomorrow) with a noun (birthday).

Directions: Circle the linking verbs. Underline the two words that are linked by the verb. The first one has been done for you.

1. Columbus is the capital of Ohio.
2. By bedtime, Nicole was bored.
3. Andy will be the captain of our team.
4. Tuesday is the first day of the month.
5. I hate to say this, but we are lost.
6. Ask him if the water is cold.
7. By the time I finished my paper, it was late.
8. Spaghetti is my favorite dinner.
9. The children were afraid of the big truck.
10. Karen will be a good president of our class.
11. These lessons are helpful.
12. Was that report due today?

15

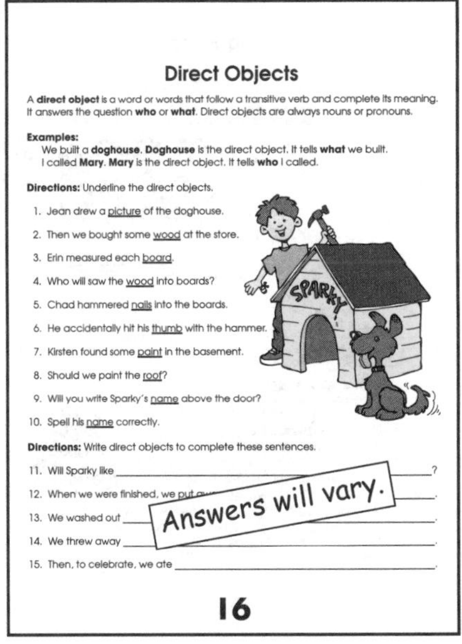

Direct Objects

A **direct object** is a word or words that follow a transitive verb and complete its meaning. It answers the question **who** or **what**. Direct objects are always nouns or pronouns.

Examples:
We built a **doghouse**. **Doghouse** is the direct object. It tells **what** we built.
I called **Mary**. **Mary** is the direct object. It tells **who** I called.

Directions: Underline the direct objects.

1. Jean drew a picture of the doghouse.
2. Then we bought some wood at the store.
3. Erin measured each board.
4. Who will saw the wood into boards?
5. Chad hammered nails into the boards.
6. He accidentally hit his thumb with the hammer.
7. Kirsten found some paint in the basement.
8. Should we paint the roof?
9. Will you write Sparky's name above the door?
10. Spell his name correctly.

Directions: Write direct objects to complete these sentences.

11. Will Sparky like __________?
12. When we were finished, we put __________.
13. We washed out __________.
14. We threw away __________.
15. Then, to celebrate, we ate __________.

Answers will vary.

16

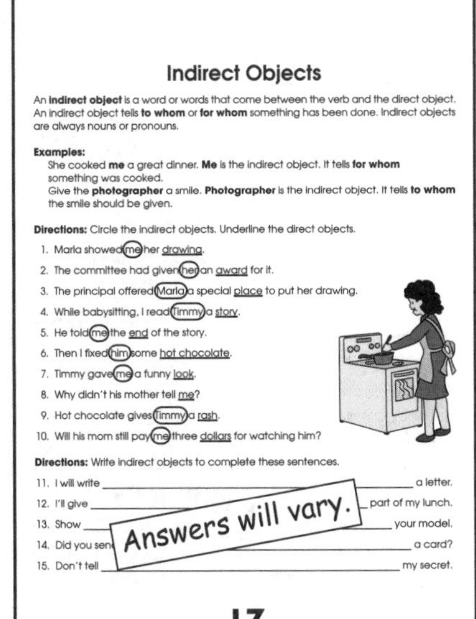

Indirect Objects

An **indirect object** is a word or words that come between the verb and the direct object. An indirect object tells **to whom** or **for whom** something has been done. Indirect objects are always nouns or pronouns.

Examples:
She cooked **me** a great dinner. **Me** is the indirect object. It tells **for whom** something was cooked.
Give the **photographer** a smile. **Photographer** is the indirect object. It tells **to whom** the smile should be given.

Directions: Circle the indirect objects. Underline the direct objects.

1. Maria showed me her drawing.
2. The committee had given her an award for it.
3. The principal offered Maria a special place to put her drawing.
4. While babysitting, I read Timmy a story.
5. He told me the end of the story.
6. Then I fixed him some hot chocolate.
7. Timmy gave me a funny look.
8. Why didn't his mother tell me?
9. Hot chocolate gives Timmy a rash.
10. Will his mom still pay me three dollars for watching him?

Directions: Write indirect objects to complete these sentences.

11. I will write __________ a letter.
12. I'll give __________ part of my lunch.
13. Show __________ your model.
14. Did you send __________ a card?
15. Don't tell __________ my secret.

Answers will vary.

17

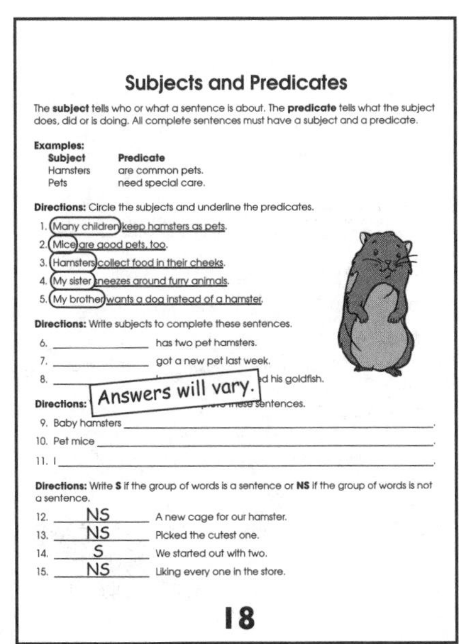

Subjects and Predicates

The **subject** tells who or what a sentence is about. The **predicate** tells what the subject does, did or is doing. All complete sentences must have a subject and a predicate.

Examples:

Subject	Predicate
Hamsters	are common pets.
Pets	need special care.

Directions: Circle the subjects and underline the predicates.

1. Many children keep hamsters as pets.
2. Mice are good pets, too.
3. Hamsters collect food in their cheeks.
4. My sister sneezes around furry animals.
5. My brother wants a dog instead of a hamster.

Directions: Write subjects to complete these sentences.

6. __________ has two pet hamsters.
7. __________ got a new pet last week.
8. __________ d his goldfish.

Directions: __________ sentences.

9. Baby hamsters __________.
10. Pet mice __________.
11. I __________.

Answers will vary.

Directions: Write **S** if the group of words is a sentence or **NS** if the group of words is not a sentence.

12. NS A new cage for our hamster.
13. NS Picked the cutest one.
14. S We started out with two.
15. NS Liking every one in the store.

18

©2006 Carson-Dellosa Publishing

Complete Sentences

A sentence which does not contain both a subject and a predicate is called a **fragment**.

Directions: Write **C** if the sentence is complete or **F** if it is a fragment.

1. C My mother and I hope to go to the mall this afternoon.
2. F To get shoes.
3. C We both need a new pair of tennis shoes.
4. F Maybe blue and white.
5. C Mom wants a pair of white shoes.
6. C That seems rather boring to me.
7. C There are many shoe stores in the mall.
8. F Sure to be a large selection.
9. C Tennis shoes are very expensive.
10. C My last pair cost $72.00!

Directions: Write the missing subject or predicate for these sentences.

11. ______ decided to go for hamburgers.
12. We ______.
13. My parents ______.
14. One day so ______.
15. My favorite subject in school ______.
16. ______ went fishing on Sunday.

Answers will vary.

19

Pronouns as Subjects

A **pronoun** is a word that takes the place of a noun. The pronouns **I**, **we**, **he**, **she**, **it**, **you** and **they** can be the subjects of a sentence.

Examples:
I left the house early.
You need to be more careful.
She dances well.

A pronoun must be singular if the noun it replaces is singular. A pronoun must be plural if the noun it replaces is plural. **He**, **she** and **it** are singular pronouns. **We** and **they** are plural pronouns. **You** is both singular and plural.

Examples:
Tina practiced playing the piano. **She** plays well.
Jim and I are studying Africa. **We** made a map of it.
The children clapped loudly. **They** liked the clown.

Directions: Write the correct pronouns.

1. Bobcats hunt at night. They are not seen during the day.
2. The mother bobcat usually has babies during February or March. She may have two litters a year.
3. The father bobcat stays away when the babies are first born. Later, he helps find food for them.
4. We have a new assignment. It is a project about bobcats.
5. My group gathered pictures of bobcats. We made a display.
6. Jennifer wrote our report. She used my notes.

Directions: Circle the pronouns that do not match the nouns they replace. Then write the correct pronouns on the lines.

7. Two boys saw a bobcat. (He) told us what happened. They
8. Then we saw a film. (They) showed bobcats climbing trees. It

20

Prepositions

A **preposition** is a word that comes before a noun or pronoun and shows the relationship of that noun or pronoun to other words in the sentence.

The **object of a preposition** is a noun or pronoun that follows a preposition and completes its meaning. A **prepositional phrase** includes a preposition and the object(s) of the preposition.

Examples:
The girl **with red hair** spoke first.
With is the preposition.
Hair is the object of the preposition.
With red hair is a prepositional phrase.

In addition to being subjects, direct and indirect objects, nouns and pronouns can also be objects of prepositions.

Prepositions						
across	below	from	near	over	to	on
by	through	in	under	off	with	of
after	before	for	between	beyond	at	down

Directions: Underline the prepositional phrases in these sentences. Circle the prepositions. The first sentence has been done for you.

1. The name (of) our street is Redsail Court.
2. We have lived (in) our house (for) three years.
3. (In) our family, we eat a lot (of) hamburgers.
4. We like hamburgers (on) toasted buns (with) mustard.
5. Sometimes we eat (in) the living room (in) front (of) the TV.
6. (In) the summer, we have picnics (in) the backyard.
7. The ants crawl (into) our food and (into) our clothes.
8. (Behind) our house is a park (with) swings.
9. Kids (from) the neighborhood walk (through) our yard (to) the park.
10. Sometimes they cut (across) Mom's garden and stomp (on) her beans.
11. Mom says we need a tall fence (without) a gate.
12. (With) a fence (around) our yard, we could get a dog!

21

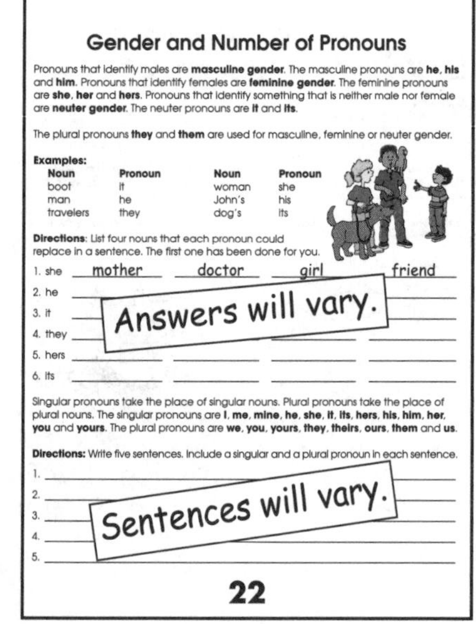

Gender and Number of Pronouns

Pronouns that identify males are **masculine gender**. The masculine pronouns are **he**, **his** and **him**. Pronouns that identify females are **feminine gender**. The feminine pronouns are **she**, **her** and **hers**. Pronouns that identify something that is neither male nor female are **neuter gender**. The neuter pronouns are **it** and **its**.

The plural pronouns **they** and **them** are used for masculine, feminine or neuter gender.

Examples:

Noun	Pronoun	Noun	Pronoun
boot	it	woman	she
man	he	John's	his
travelers	they	dog's	its

Directions: List four nouns that each pronoun could replace in a sentence. The first one has been done for you.

1. she mother doctor girl friend
2. he
3. it
4. they
5. hers
6. its

Answers will vary.

Singular pronouns take the place of singular nouns. Plural pronouns take the place of plural nouns. The singular pronouns are **I**, **me**, **mine**, **he**, **she**, **it**, **its**, **hers**, **his**, **him**, **her**, **you** and **yours**. The plural pronouns are **we**, **you**, **yours**, **they**, **theirs**, **ours**, **them** and **us**.

Directions: Write five sentences. Include a singular and a plural pronoun in each sentence.

1.
2.
3.
4.
5.

Sentences will vary.

22

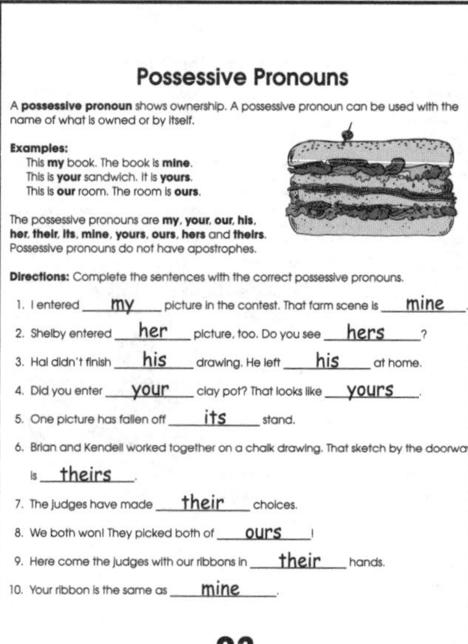

Possessive Pronouns

A **possessive pronoun** shows ownership. A possessive pronoun can be used with the name of what is owned or by itself.

Examples:
This **my** book. The book is **mine**.
This is **your** sandwich. It is **yours**.
This is **our** room. The room is **ours**.

The possessive pronouns are **my**, **your**, **our**, **his**, **her**, **their**, **its**, **mine**, **yours**, **ours**, **hers** and **theirs**. Possessive pronouns do not have apostrophes.

Directions: Complete the sentences with the correct possessive pronouns.

1. I entered my picture in the contest. That farm scene is mine.
2. Shelby entered her picture, too. Do you see hers?
3. Hal didn't finish his drawing. He left his at home.
4. Did you enter your clay pot? That looks like yours.
5. One picture has fallen off its stand.
6. Brian and Kendell worked together on a chalk drawing. That sketch by the doorway is theirs.
7. The judges have made their choices.
8. We both won! They picked both of ours!
9. Here come the judges with our ribbons in their hands.
10. Your ribbon is the same as mine.

23

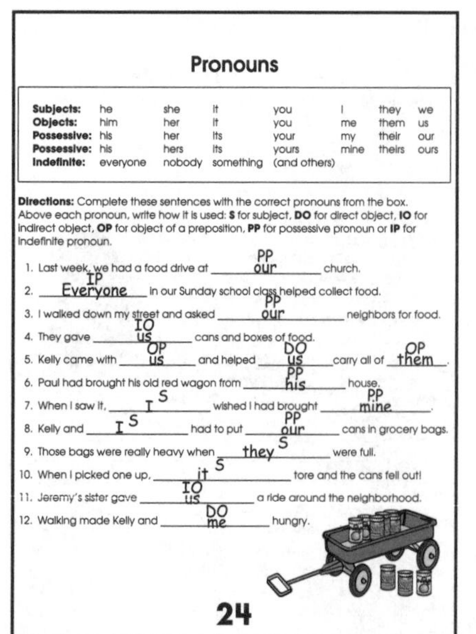

Pronouns

Subjects:	he	she	it	you	I	they	we
Objects:	him	her	it	you	me	them	us
Possessive:	his	her	its	your	my	their	our
Possessive:	his	hers	its	yours	mine	theirs	ours
Indefinite:	everyone	nobody	something	(and others)			

Directions: Complete these sentences with the correct pronouns from the box. Above each pronoun, write how it is used: **S** for subject, **DO** for direct object, **IO** for indirect object, **OP** for object of a preposition, **PP** for possessive pronoun or **IP** for indefinite pronoun.

1. Last week, we had a food drive at our (PP) church.
2. Everyone (IP) in our Sunday school class helped collect food.
3. I walked down my street and asked our (PP) neighbors for food.
4. They gave us (IO) cans and boxes of food.
5. Kelly came with us (OP) and helped us (DO) carry all of them (OP).
6. Paul had brought his old red wagon from his (PP) house.
7. When I saw it, I (S) wished I had brought mine (PP).
8. Kelly and I (S) had to put our (PP) cans in grocery bags.
9. Those bags were really heavy when they (S) were full.
10. When I picked one up, it (S) tore and the cans fell out!
11. Jeremy's sister gave us (IO) a ride around the neighborhood.
12. Walking made Kelly and me (DO) hungry.

24

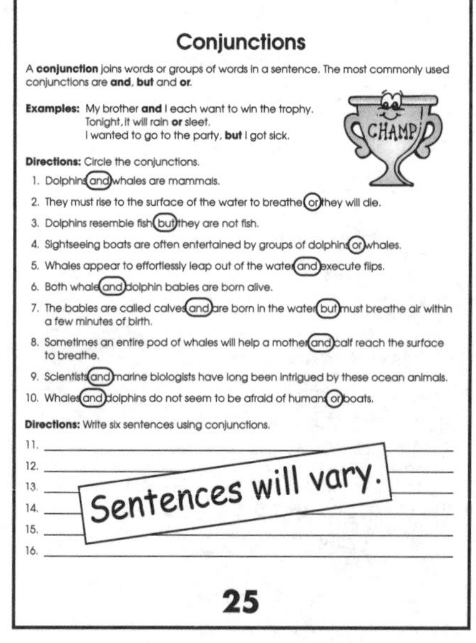

Conjunctions

A **conjunction** joins words or groups of words in a sentence. The most commonly used conjunctions are **and**, **but** and **or**.

Examples: My brother **and** I each want to win the trophy.
Tonight, it will rain **or** sleet.
I wanted to go to the party, **but** I got sick.

Directions: Circle the conjunctions.

1. Dolphins (and) whales are mammals.
2. They must rise to the surface of the water to breathe (or) they will die.
3. Dolphins resemble fish (but) they are not fish.
4. Sightseeing boats are often entertained by groups of dolphins (or) whales.
5. Whales appear to effortlessly leap out of the water (and) execute flips.
6. Both whale (and) dolphin babies are born alive.
7. The babies are called calves (and) are born in the water (but) must breathe air within a few minutes of birth.
8. Sometimes an entire pod of whales will help a mother (and) calf reach the surface to breathe.
9. Scientists (and) marine biologists have long been intrigued by these ocean animals.
10. Whales (and) dolphins do not seem to be afraid of humans (or) boats.

Directions: Write six sentences using conjunctions.

11.
12.
13.
14.
15.
16.

Sentences will vary.

25

©2006 Carson-Dellosa Publishing

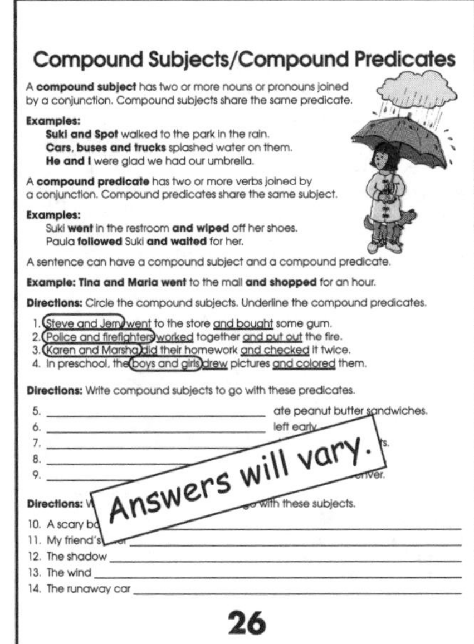

Compound Subjects/Compound Predicates

A **compound subject** has two or more nouns or pronouns joined by a conjunction. Compound subjects share the same predicate.

Examples:
Suki and Spot walked to the park in the rain.
Cars, buses and trucks splashed water on them.
He and I were glad we had our umbrella.

A **compound predicate** has two or more verbs joined by a conjunction. Compound predicates share the same subject.

Examples:
Suki **went** in the restroom **and wiped** off her shoes.
Paula **followed** Suki **and waited** for her.

A sentence can have a compound subject and a compound predicate.

Example: Tina and Maria went to the mall **and shopped** for an hour.

Directions: Circle the compound subjects. Underline the compound predicates.

1. Steve and Jerry went to the store and bought some gum.
2. Police and firefighters worked together and put out the fire.
3. Karen and Marsha did their homework and checked it twice.
4. In preschool, the boys and girls drew pictures and colored them.

Directions: Write compound subjects to go with these predicates.

5. ______ ate peanut butter sandwiches.
6. ______ left early.
7. ______ ...s.
8. ______
9. ______ ...river.

Answers will vary.

Directions: W... ...with these subjects.

10. A scary bo... ______
11. My friend's... ______
12. The shadow ______
13. The wind ______
14. The runaway car ______

26

Combining Subjects

Too many short sentences make writing sound choppy. Often, we can combine sentences with different subjects and the same predicate to make one sentence with a compound subject.

Example:
Lisa tried out for the play. Todd tried out for the play.
Compound subject: Lisa and Todd tried out for the play.

When sentences have different subjects and different predicates, we cannot combine them this way. Each subject and predicate must stay together. Two short sentences can be combined with a conjunction.

Examples:
Lisa got a part in the play. Todd will help make scenery.
Lisa got a part in the play, and Todd will help make scenery.

Directions: If a pair of sentences share the same predicate, combine them with compound subjects. If the sentences have different subjects and predicates, combine them using **and**.

1. Rachel read a book about explorers. Eric read the same book about explorers.
Rachel and Eric read a book about explorers.
2. Rachel really liked the book. Eric agreed with her.
Rachel really liked the book, and Eric agreed with her.
3. Vicki went to the basketball game last night. Dan went to the basketball game, too.
Vicki and Dan went to the basketball game last night.
4. Vicki lost her coat. Dan missed his ride home.
Vicki lost her coat, and Dan missed his ride home.
5. My uncle planted corn in the garden. My mother planted corn in the garden.
My uncle and my mother planted corn in the garden.
6. Isaac helped with the food drive last week. Amy helped with the food drive, too.
Isaac and Amy helped with the food drive last week.

27

Combining Predicates

If short sentences have the same subject and different predicates, we can combine them into one sentence with a compound predicate.

Example:
Andy got up late this morning.
He nearly missed the school bus.
Compound predicate: Andy got up late this morning and nearly missed the school bus.

The pronoun **he** takes the place of Andy in the second sentence, so the subjects are the same and can be combined.

When two sentences have different subjects and different predicates, we cannot combine them this way. Two short sentences can be combined with a conjunction.

Examples:
Andy got up late this morning. Cindy woke up early.
Andy got up late this morning, but Cindy woke up early.

Directions: If the pair of sentences share the same subject, combine them with compound predicates. If the sentences have different subjects and predicates, combine them using **and** or **but**.

1. Kyle practiced pitching all winter. Kyle became the pitcher for his team.
Kyle practiced pitching all winter and became the pitcher for his team.
2. Kisha studied two hours for her history test. Angela watched TV.
Kisha studied two hours for her history test, but Angela watched TV.
3. Jeff had an ear ache. He took medicine four times a day.
Jeff had an earache and took medicine four times a day.
4. Nikki found a new hair style. Melissa didn't like that style.
Nikki found a new hair style, but Melissa didn't like that style.
5. Kirby buys his lunch every day. Sean brings his lunch from home.
Kirby buys his lunch everyday, but Sean brings his lunch from home.

28

Run-On Sentences

A **run-on sentence** occurs when two or more sentences are joined together without the correct punctuation. A run-on sentence must be divided into two or more separate sentences.

Example:
Run-on: On Tuesday my family went to the amusement park but unfortunately it rained and we got wet and it took hours for our clothes to dry.
Correct: On Tuesday, my family went to the amusement park. Unfortunately, it rained and we got wet. It took hours for our clothes to dry.

Directions: Rewrite these run-on sentences correctly.

1. I have a dog named Boxer and a cat named Phoebe and they are both well-behaved and friendly.
I have a dog named Boxer and a cat named Phoebe. They are both friendly and well-behaved.
2. Jacob's basketball coach makes the team run for 20 minutes each practice and then he makes them play a full game and afterwards he makes them do 50 push-ups and 100 sit-ups.
Jacob's basketball coach makes the team run for 20 minutes each practice. Then he makes them play a full game. Afterwards, he makes them do 50 push-ups and 100 sit-ups.
3. My family members each enjoy different hobbies Mom likes to paint Dad likes to read I like to play sports and my younger sister likes to build model airplanes although I think they are too hard.
My family members each enjoy different hobbies. Mom likes to paint. Dad likes to read. I like to play sports. My younger sister likes to build model airplanes, although I think they are too hard.

29

Statements and Questions

A **statement** is a sentence that tells something. It ends with a period (.).

A **question** is a sentence that asks something. It ends with a question mark (?).

Examples:
Statement: Shari is walking to school today.
Question: Is Shari walking to school today?

In some questions, the subject comes between two parts of the verb. In the examples below, the subjects are underlined. The verbs and the rest of the predicates are bold.

Examples:
Is Steve **coming with us**?
Who **will be there**?
Which one did you **select**?

To find the predicate, turn a question into a statement.

Example: Is Steve coming with us? Steve is coming with us.

Directions: Write **S** for statement or **Q** for question. Put a period after the statements and a question mark after the questions.

S 1. Today is the day for our field trip.
Q 2. How are we going to get there?
S 3. The bus will take us.
Q 4. Is there room for everyone?
Q 5. Who forgot to bring a lunch?
S 6. I'll save you a seat.

Directions: Circle the subjects and underline all parts of the predicates.

7. Do you like field trips?
8. Did you bring your coat?
9. Will it be cold there?
10. Do you see my gloves anywhere?
11. Is anyone sitting with you?
12. Does the bus driver have a map?
13. Are all the roads this bumpy?

30

Commands, Requests and Exclamations

A **command** is a sentence that orders someone to do something. It ends with a period or an exclamation mark (!).

A **request** is a sentence that asks someone to do something. It ends with a period or a question mark (?).

An **exclamation** is a sentence that shows strong feeling. It ends with an exclamation mark (!).

Examples:
Command: Stay in your seat.
Request: Would you please pass the salt?
Please pass the salt.
Exclamation: Call the police!

In the first and last two sentences in the examples, the subject is not stated. The subject is understood to be **you**.

Directions: Write **C** if the sentence is a command, **R** if it is a request and **E** if it is an exclamation. Put the correct punctuation at the end of each sentence.

C 1. Look both ways before you cross the street.
R 2. Please go to the store and buy some bread for us.
E 3. The house is on fire!
R 4. Would you hand me the glue?
C 5. Don't step there.
C 6. Write your name at the top of the page.
R 7. Please close the door.
R 8. Would you answer the phone?
E 9. Watch out!
C 10. Take one card from each pile.

31

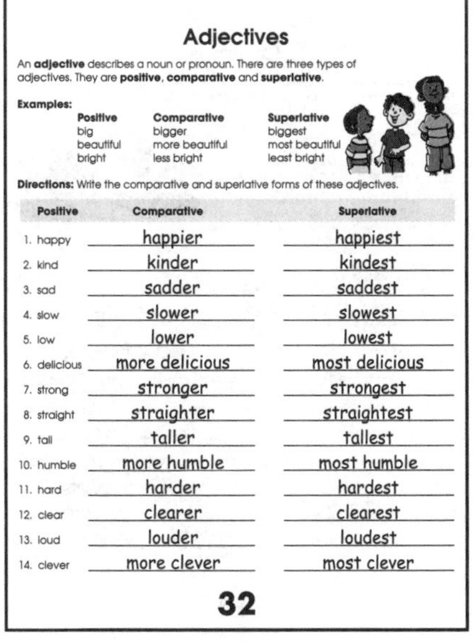

Adjectives

An **adjective** describes a noun or pronoun. There are three types of adjectives. They are **positive**, **comparative** and **superlative**.

Examples:

Positive	Comparative	Superlative
big	bigger	biggest
beautiful	more beautiful	most beautiful
bright	less bright	least bright

Directions: Write the comparative and superlative forms of these adjectives.

Positive	Comparative	Superlative
1. happy	happier	happiest
2. kind	kinder	kindest
3. sad	sadder	saddest
4. slow	slower	slowest
5. low	lower	lowest
6. delicious	more delicious	most delicious
7. strong	stronger	strongest
8. straight	straighter	straightest
9. tall	taller	tallest
10. humble	more humble	most humble
11. hard	harder	hardest
12. clear	clearer	clearest
13. loud	louder	loudest
14. clever	more clever	most clever

32

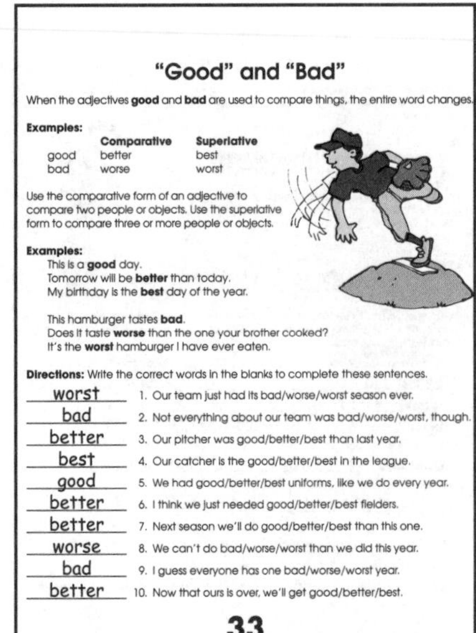

"Good" and "Bad"

When the adjectives **good** and **bad** are used to compare things, the entire word changes.

Examples:

	Comparative	**Superlative**
good	better	best
bad	worse	worst

Use the comparative form of an adjective to compare two people or objects. Use the superlative form to compare three or more people or objects.

Examples:
This is a **good** day.
Tomorrow will be **better** than today.
My birthday is the **best** day of the year.

This hamburger tastes **bad**.
Does it taste **worse** than the one your brother cooked?
It's the **worst** hamburger I have ever eaten.

Directions: Write the correct words in the blanks to complete these sentences.

worst 1. Our team just had its bad/worse/worst season ever.
bad 2. Not everything about our team was bad/worse/worst, though.
better 3. Our pitcher was good/better/best than last year.
best 4. Our catcher is the good/better/best in the league.
good 5. We had good/better/best uniforms, like we do every year.
better 6. I think we just needed good/better/best fielders.
better 7. Next season we'll do good/better/best than this one.
worse 8. We can't do bad/worse/worst than we did this year.
bad 9. I guess everyone has one bad/worse/worst year.
better 10. Now that ours is over, we'll get good/better/best.

33

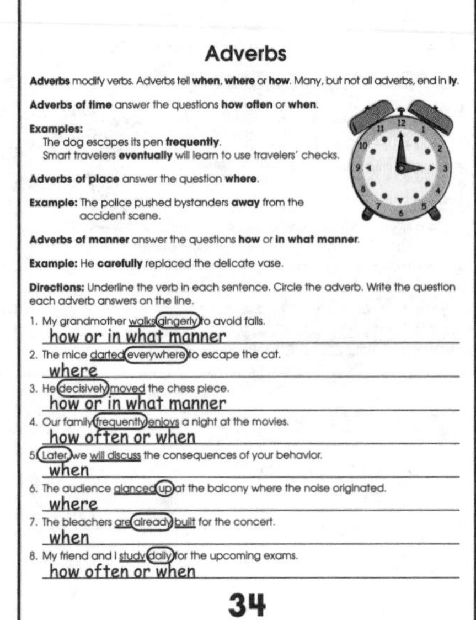

Adverbs

Adverbs modify verbs. Adverbs tell **when**, **where** or **how**. Many, but not all adverbs, end in **ly**.

Adverbs of time answer the questions **how often** or **when**.

Examples:
The dog escapes its pen **frequently**.
Smart travelers **eventually** will learn to use travelers' checks.

Adverbs of place answer the question **where**.

Example: The police pushed bystanders **away** from the accident scene.

Adverbs of manner answer the questions **how** or **in what manner**.

Example: He **carefully** replaced the delicate vase.

Directions: Underline the verb in each sentence. Circle the adverb. Write the question each adverb answers on the line.

1. My grandmother walks gingerly to avoid falls.
how or in what manner
2. The mice darted everywhere to escape the cat.
where
3. He decisively moved the chess piece.
how or in what manner
4. Our family frequently enjoys a night at the movies.
how often or when
5. Later we will discuss the consequences of your behavior.
when
6. The audience glanced up at the balcony where the noise originated.
where
7. The bleachers are already built for the concert.
when
8. My friend and I study daily for the upcoming exams.
how often or when

34

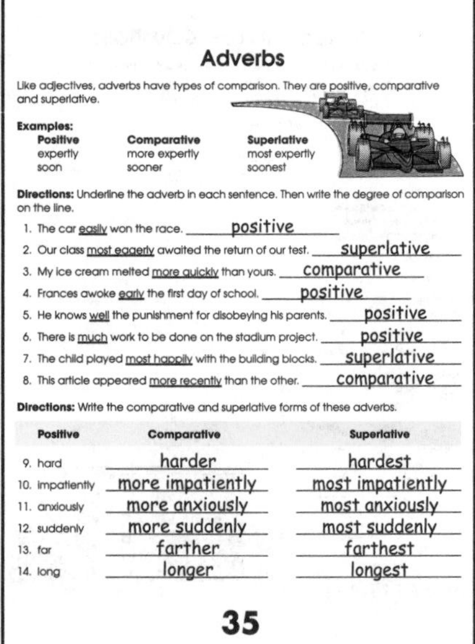

Adverbs

Like adjectives, adverbs have types of comparison. They are positive, comparative and superlative.

Examples:

Positive	**Comparative**	**Superlative**
expertly	more expertly	most expertly
soon	sooner	soonest

Directions: Underline the adverb in each sentence. Then write the degree of comparison on the line.

1. The car easily won the race. positive
2. Our class most eagerly awaited the return of our test. superlative
3. My ice cream melted more quickly than yours. comparative
4. Frances awoke early the first day of school. positive
5. He knows well the punishment for disobeying his parents. positive
6. There is much work to be done on the stadium project. positive
7. The child played most happily with the building blocks. superlative
8. This article appeared more recently than the other. comparative

Directions: Write the comparative and superlative forms of these adverbs.

Positive	**Comparative**	**Superlative**
9. hard	harder	hardest
10. impatiently	more impatiently	most impatiently
11. anxiously	more anxiously	most anxiously
12. suddenly	more suddenly	most suddenly
13. far	farther	farthest
14. long	longer	longest

35

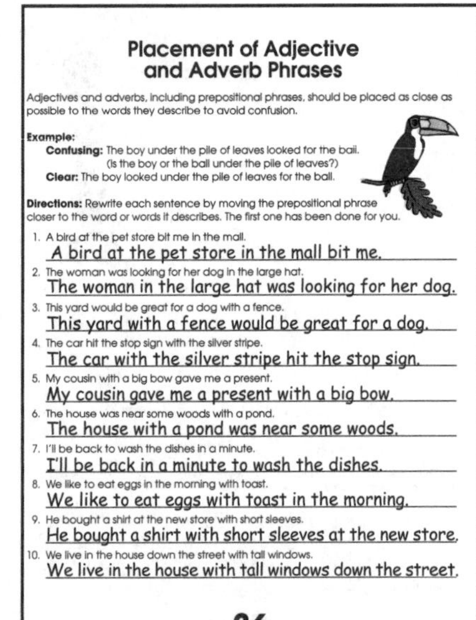

Placement of Adjective and Adverb Phrases

Adjectives and adverbs, including prepositional phrases, should be placed as close as possible to the words they describe to avoid confusion.

Example:
Confusing: The boy under the pile of leaves looked for the ball. (Is the boy or the ball under the pile of leaves?)
Clear: The boy looked under the pile of leaves for the ball.

Directions: Rewrite each sentence by moving the prepositional phrase closer to the word or words it describes. The first one has been done for you.

1. A bird at the pet store bit me in the mall.
A bird at the pet store in the mall bit me.
2. The woman was looking for her dog in the large hat.
The woman in the large hat was looking for her dog.
3. This yard would be great for a dog with a fence.
This yard with a fence would be great for a dog.
4. The car hit the stop sign with the silver stripe.
The car with the silver stripe hit the stop sign.
5. My cousin with a big bow gave me a present.
My cousin gave me a present with a big bow.
6. The house was near some woods with a pond.
The house with a pond was near some woods.
7. I'll be back to wash the dishes in a minute.
I'll be back in a minute to wash the dishes.
8. We like to eat eggs in the morning with toast.
We like to eat eggs with toast in the morning.
9. He bought a shirt at the new store with short sleeves.
He bought a shirt with short sleeves at the new store.
10. We live in the house down the street with tall windows.
We live in the house with tall windows down the street.

36

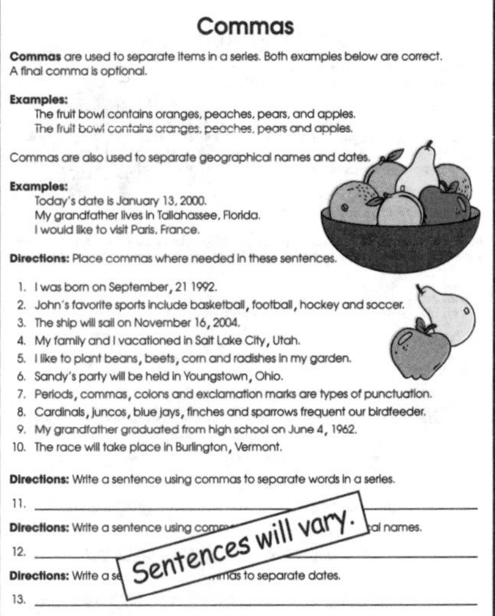

Commas

Commas are used to separate items in a series. Both examples below are correct. A final comma is optional.

Examples:
The fruit bowl contains oranges, peaches, pears, and apples.
The fruit bowl contains oranges, peaches, pears and apples.

Commas are also used to separate geographical names and dates.

Examples:
Today's date is January 13, 2000.
My grandfather lives in Tallahassee, Florida.
I would like to visit Paris, France.

Directions: Place commas where needed in these sentences.

1. I was born on September, 21 1992.
2. John's favorite sports include basketball, football, hockey and soccer.
3. The ship will sail on November 16, 2004.
4. My family and I vacationed in Salt Lake City, Utah.
5. I like to plant beans, beets, corn and radishes in my garden.
6. Sandy's party will be held in Youngstown, Ohio.
7. Periods, commas, colons and exclamation marks are types of punctuation.
8. Cardinals, juncos, blue jays, finches and sparrows frequent our birdfeeder.
9. My grandfather graduated from high school on June 4, 1962.
10. The race will take place in Burlington, Vermont.

Directions: Write a sentence using commas to separate words in a series.

11. ____

Directions: Write a sentence using comm... ...al names.

12. ____

Directions: Write a se... ...mas to separate dates.

13. ____

Sentences will vary.

37

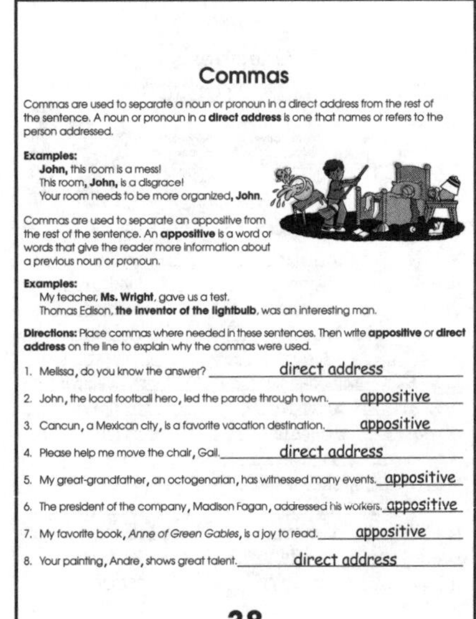

Commas

Commas are used to separate a noun or pronoun in a direct address from the rest of the sentence. A noun or pronoun in a **direct address** is one that names or refers to the person addressed.

Examples:
John, this room is a mess!
This room, **John,** is a disgrace!
Your room needs to be more organized, **John**.

Commas are used to separate an appositive from the rest of the sentence. An **appositive** is a word or words that give the reader more information about a previous noun or pronoun.

Examples:
My teacher, **Ms. Wright**, gave us a test.
Thomas Edison, **the inventor of the lightbulb**, was an interesting man.

Directions: Place commas where needed in these sentences. Then write **appositive** or **direct address** on the line to explain why the commas were used.

1. Melissa, do you know the answer? direct address
2. John, the local football hero, led the parade through town. appositive
3. Cancun, a Mexican city, is a favorite vacation destination. appositive
4. Please help me move the chair, Gail. direct address
5. My great-grandfather, an octogenarian, has witnessed many events. appositive
6. The president of the company, Madison Fagan, addressed his workers. appositive
7. My favorite book, *Anne of Green Gables*, is a joy to read. appositive
8. Your painting, Andre, shows great talent. direct address

38

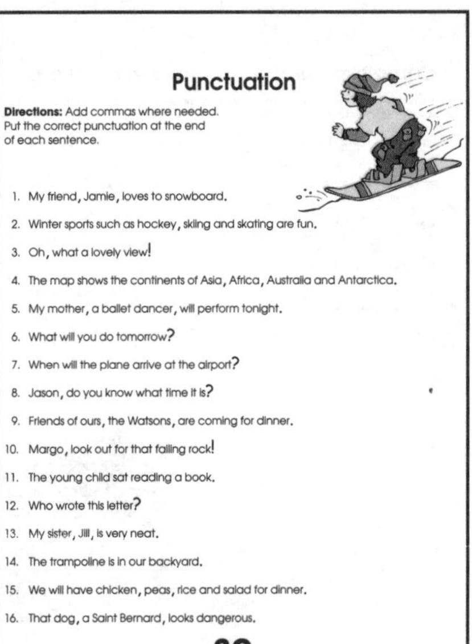

Punctuation

Directions: Add commas where needed. Put the correct punctuation at the end of each sentence.

1. My friend, Jamie, loves to snowboard.
2. Winter sports such as hockey, skiing and skating are fun.
3. Oh, what a lovely view!
4. The map shows the continents of Asia, Africa, Australia and Antarctica.
5. My mother, a ballet dancer, will perform tonight.
6. What will you do tomorrow?
7. When will the plane arrive at the airport?
8. Jason, do you know what time it is?
9. Friends of ours, the Watsons, are coming for dinner.
10. Margo, look out for that falling rock!
11. The young child sat reading a book.
12. Who wrote this letter?
13. My sister, Jill, is very neat.
14. The trampoline is in our backyard.
15. We will have chicken, peas, rice and salad for dinner.
16. That dog, a Saint Bernard, looks dangerous.

39

 ©2006 Carson-Dellosa Publishing

Quotation Marks

When a person's exact words are used in a sentence, **quotation marks** (**" "**) are used to identify those words. Commas are used to set off the quotation from the rest of the sentence. End punctuation is placed inside the final quotation marks.

Examples:
"When are we leaving?" Joe asked.
Marci shouted, "Go, team!"

When a sentence is interrupted by words that are not part of the quotation (he said, she answered, etc.), they are not included in the quotation marks. Note how commas are used in the next example.

Example: "I am sorry," the man announced, "for my rude behavior."

Directions: Place quotation marks, commas and other punctuation where needed in the sentences below.

1. "Watch out!" yelled Dad.
2. Angela said, "I don't know how you can eat Brussels sprouts, Ted."
3. "Put on your coats," said Mom. "We'll be leaving in 10 minutes."
4. "Did you hear the assignment?" asked Joan.
5. Jim shouted, "This game is driving me up the wall!"
6. After examining our dog, the veterinarian said, "He looks healthy and strong."
7. The toddlers both wailed, "We want ice cream!"
8. The judge announced to the swimmers, "Take your places."
9. Upon receiving the award, the actor said, "I'd like to thank my friends and family."
10. "These are my favorite chips," said Becky.
11. "This test is too hard," moaned the class.
12. When their relay team came in first place, the runners shouted, "Hooray!"
13. "Where shall we go on vacation this year?" Dad asked.
14. As we walked past the machinery, the noise was deafening. "Cover your ears," said Mom.
15. "Fire!" yelled the chef as his pan ignited.
16. "I love basketball," my little brother stated.

40

Capitalization

Directions: Write **C** if capital letters are used correctly or **X** if they are used incorrectly.

X 1. Who will win the election for Mayor in November?
C 2. Tom Johnson used to be a police officer.
X 3. He announced on monday that he wants to be mayor.
C 4. My father said he would vote for Tom.
C 5. Mom and my sister Judy haven't decided yet.
C 6. They will vote at our school.
X 7. Every Fall and Spring they put up voting booths there.
C 8. I hope the new mayor will do something about our river.
X 9. That River is full of chemicals.
C 10. I'm glad our water doesn't come from Raven River.
X 11. In late Summer, the river actually stinks.
X 12. Is every river in our State so dirty?
C 13. Scientists check the water every so often.
C 14. Some professors from the college even examined it.
X 15. That is getting to be a very educated River!

Directions: Write sentences that include:

16. A person's title that should be capitalized.
17. The name of a place that should be
18. The name of a tim ... holiday) that should be capitalized.

Answers will vary.

41

Combining Sentences

When the subjects are the same, sentences can be combined by using appositives.

Examples:
Tony likes to play basketball. Tony is my neighbor.
Tony, **my neighbor**, likes to play basketball.

Ms. Herman was sick today. Ms. Herman is our math teacher.
Ms. Herman, **our math teacher**, was sick today.

Appositives are set off from the rest of the sentence with commas.

Directions: Use commas and appositives to combine the pairs of sentences.

1. Julie has play practice today. Julie is my sister.
Julie, my sister, has play practice today.
2. Greg fixed my bicycle. Greg is my cousin.
Greg, my cousin, fixed my bicycle.
3. Mr. Scott told us where to meet. Mr. Scott is our coach.
Mr. Scott, our coach, told us where to meet.
4. Tiffany is moving to Detroit. Tiffany is my neighbor.
Tiffany, my neighbor, is moving to Detroit.
5. Kyle has the flu. Kyle is my brother.
Kyle, my brother, has the flu.
6. My favorite football team is playing tonight. Houston is my favorite team.
My favorite football team, Houston, is playing tonight.
7. Bonnie Pryor will be at our school next week. Bonnie Pryor is a famous author.
Bonnie Pryor, a famous author, will be at our school next week.
8. Our neighborhood is having a garage sale. Our neighborhood is the North End.
Our neighborhood, the North End, is having a garage sale.

42

"Who" Clauses

A **clause** is a group of words with a subject and a verb. When the subject of two sentences is the same person or people, the sentences can sometimes be combined with a "who" clause.

Examples:
Mindy likes animals. Mindy feeds the squirrels.
Mindy, **who likes animals**, feeds the squirrels.

A "who" clause is set off from the rest of the sentence with commas.

Directions: Combine the pairs of sentences, using "who" clauses.

1. Teddy was late to school. Teddy was sorry later.
Teddy, who was late to school, was sorry later.
2. Our principal is retiring. Our principal will be 65 this year.
Our principal, who will be 65 this year, is retiring.
3. Michael won the contest. Michael will receive an award.
Michael, who won the contest, will receive an award.
4. Charlene lives next door. Charlene has three cats.
Charlene, who lives next door, has three cats.
5. Burt drew that picture. Burt takes art lessons.
Burt, who drew that picture, takes art lessons.
6. Marta was elected class president. Marta gave a speech.
Marta, who was elected class president, gave a speech.
7. Amy broke her arm. Amy has to wear a cast for 6 weeks.
Amy, who broke her arm, has to wear a cast for 6 weeks.
8. Dr. Bank fixed my tooth. He said it would feel better soon.
Dr. Bank, who fixed my tooth, said it would feel better soon.

43

"Which" Clauses

When the subject of two sentences is the same thing or things, the sentences can sometimes be combined with a "which" clause.

Examples:
The guppy was first called "the millions fish." The guppy was later named after Reverend Robert Guppy in 1866.
The guppy, **which was first called "the millions fish,"** was later named after Reverend Robert Guppy in 1866.

A "which" clause is set off from the rest of the sentence with commas.

Directions: Combine the pairs of sentences using "which" clauses.

1. Guppies, which also used to be called rainbow fish, were brought to Germany in 1908.
2. The male guppy, which is about 1 inch long, is smaller than the female.
3. The guppies' colors, which range from red to violet, are brighter in the males.
4. Baby guppies, which hatch from eggs inside the mothers' bodies, are born alive.
5. The young, which are usually born at night, are called "fry."
6. Female guppies, which have 2 to 50 fry at one time, sometimes try to eat their fry!
7. These fish, which have been studied by scientists, actually like dirty water.
8. Wild guppies, which eat mosquito eggs, help control the mosquito population.

44

"That" Clauses

When the subject of two sentences is the same thing or things, the sentences can sometimes be combined with a "that" clause. We use **that** instead of **which** when the clause is very important in the sentence.

Examples:
The store is near our house. The store was closed.
The store **that is near our house** was closed.

The words "**that is near our house**" are very important in the combined sentence. They tell the reader which store was closed. A "that" clause is not set off from the rest of the sentence with commas.

Examples:
Pete's store is near our house. Pete's store was closed.
Pete's store, which is near our house, was closed.

The words "**which is near our house**" are not important to the meaning of the combined sentence. The words **Pete's store** already told us which store was closed.

Directions: Combine the pairs of sentences using "that" clauses.

1. The dog lives next door. The dog chased me.
The dog that lives next door chased me.
2. The bus was taking us to the game. The bus had a flat tire.
The bus that was taking us to the game had a flat tire.
3. The fence is around the school. The fence is painted yellow.
The fence that is around the school is painted yellow.
4. The notebook had my homework in it. The notebook is lost.
The notebook that had my homework in it is lost.
5. A letter came today. The letter was from Mary.
A letter that was from Mary came today.
6. The lamp was fixed yesterday. The lamp doesn't work today.
The lamp that was fixed yesterday doesn't work today.
7. The lake is by our cabin. The lake is filled with fish.
The lake that is by our cabin is filled with fish.

45

"That" and "Which" Clauses

Directions: Combine the pairs of sentences using either a "that" or a "which" clause.

1. The TV show was on at 8:00 last night. The TV show was funny.
The TV show that was on at 8:00 last night was funny.
2. *The Snappy Show* was on at 8:00 last night. *The Snappy Show* was funny.
The Snappy Show, which was on at 8:00 last night, was funny.
3. The Main Bank is on the corner. The Main Bank is closed today.
The Main Bank, which is on the corner, is closed today.
4. The bank is on the corner. The bank is closed today.
The bank that is on the corner is closed today.
5. The bus takes Dad to work. The bus broke down.
The bus that takes Dad to work broke down.
6. The Broad Street bus takes Dad to work. The Broad Street bus broke down.
The Broad Street bus, which takes Dad to work, broke down.

46

Combining Sentences

Not every pair of sentences can be combined with "who," "which" or "that" clauses. These sentences can be combined in other ways, either with a conjunction or by renaming the subject.

Examples:

Tim couldn't go to sleep. Todd was sleeping soundly.
Tim couldn't go to sleep, **but** Todd was sleeping soundly.

The zoo keeper fed the baby ape. A crowd gathered to watch.
When the zoo keeper fed the baby ape, a crowd gathered to watch.

Directions: Combine each pair of sentences using "who," "which" or "that" clauses, by using a conjunction or by renaming the subject.

1. The box slipped off the truck. The box was filled with bottles.
   The box that was filled with bottles slipped off the truck.
2. Carolyn is our scout leader. Carolyn taught us a new game.
   Carolyn, who is our scout leader, taught us a new game.
3. The girl is 8 years old. The girl called the emergency number when her grandmother fell.
   The girl, who is 8 years old, called the emergency number when her grandmother fell.
4. The meatloaf is ready to eat. The salad isn't made yet.
   The meatloaf is ready to eat, but the salad isn't made yet.
5. The rain poured down. The rain canceled our picnic.
   The rain poured down and canceled our picnic.
6. The sixth grade class went on a field trip. The school was much quieter.
   When the sixth grade class went on a field trip, the school was much quieter.

47

"Who's" and "Whose"

Who's is a contraction for **who is**.

Whose is a possessive pronoun.

Examples:

Who's going to come?
Whose shirt is this?

To know which word to use, substitute the words "who is." If the sentence makes sense, use **who's**.

Directions: Write the correct word to complete these sentences.

who's 1. Do you know who's/whose invited to the party?
whose 2. I don't even know who's/whose house it will be at.
Whose 3. Who's/Whose towel is on the floor?
Who's 4. Who's/Whose going to drive us?
Whose 5. Who's/Whose ice cream is melting?
whose 6. I'm the person who's/whose gloves are lost.
Who's 7. Who's/Whose in your group?.
Whose 8. Who's/Whose group is first?
who's 9. Can you tell who's/whose at the door?
Whose 10. Who's/Whose friend are you?
Who's 11. Who's/Whose cooking tonight?
Whose 12. Who's/Whose cooking do you like best?

48

"Their," "There" and "They're"

Their is a possessive pronoun meaning "belonging to them."

There is an adverb that indicates place.

They're is a contraction for **they are**.

Examples:

Ron and Sue took **their** dog to the park.
They like to go **there** on Sunday afternoon.
They're probably going back next Sunday, too.

Directions: Write the correct words to complete these sentences.

their 1. All the students should bring their/there/they're books to class.
there 2. I've never been to France, but I hope to travel their/there/they're someday.
their 3. We studied how dolphins care for their/there/they're young.
they're 4. My parents are going on vacation next week, and their/there/they're taking my sister.
There 5. Their/There/They're was a lot of food at the party.
their 6. My favorite baseball team lost their/there/they're star pitcher this year.
they're 7. Those peaches look good, but their/there/they're not ripe yet.
there 8. The book is right their/there/they're on the table.

49

"Teach" and "Learn"

Teach is a verb meaning "to explain something." Teach is an irregular verb. Its past tense is **taught**.

Learn is a verb meaning "to gain information."

Examples:

Carrie will **teach** me how to play the piano.
Yesterday she **taught** me "Chopsticks."

I will **learn** a new song every week.
Yesterday I **learned** to play "Chopsticks."

Directions: Write the correct words to complete these sentences.

taught 1. My brother taught/learned me how to ice skate.
learned 2. With his help, I taught/learned in three days.
learn 3. First, I tried to teach/learn skating from a book.
learn 4. I couldn't teach/learn that way.
learn 5. You have to try it before you can really teach/learn how to do it.
teach 6. Now I'm going to teach/learn my cousin.
learned 7. My cousin already taught/learned how to roller skate.
teaching 8. I shouldn't have any trouble teaching/learning her how to ice skate.
taught 9. Who taught/learned you how to skate?
taught 10. My brother taught/learned Mom how to skate, too.
learn 11. My mother took longer to teach/learn it than I did.
teach 12. Who will he teach/learn next?
learn 13. Do you know anyone who wants to teach/learn how to ice skate?
teach 14. My brother will teach/learn you for free.
learn 15. You should teach/learn how to ice skate in the wintertime, though. The ice is a little thin in the summer!

50

"Lie" and "Lay"

Lie is a verb meaning "to rest." Lie is an intransitive verb that doesn't need a direct object.

Lay is a verb meaning "to place or put something down." Lay is a transitive verb that requires a direct object.

Examples:

Lie here for a while. (**Lie** has no direct object; **here** is an adverb.)
Lay the book here. (**Lay** has a direct object: **book**.)

Lie and lay are especially tricky because they are both irregular verbs. Notice the past tense of lie is lay!

Present tense	ing form	Past tense	Past participle
lie	lying	lay	has/have/had lain
lay	laying	laid	has/have/had laid

Examples:

I **lie** here today.
I **lay** here yesterday.
I **was lying** there for three hours.

I **lay** the baby in her bed.
I will be **laying** her down in a minute.
I **laid** her in her bed last night, too.

Directions: Write the correct words to complete these sentences.

lays 1. Shelly lies/lays a blanket on the grass.
lies 2. Then she lies/lays down in the sun.
lies 3. Her dog lies/lays there with her.
laid 4. Yesterday, Shelly lay/laid in the sun for an hour.
laying 5. The workers are lying/laying bricks for a house.
laid 6. Yesterday, they lay/laid a ton of them.
lay 7. They lie/lay one brick on top of the other.
lay 8. The bricks just lie/lay in a pile until the workers are ready for them.
lie 9. At lunchtime, some workers lie/lay down for a nap.
lay 10. Would you like to lie/lay bricks?
laid 11. Last year, my uncle lay/laid bricks for his new house.
laid 12. He was so tired every day that he lay/laid down as soon as he finished.

51

"Rise" and "Raise"

Rise is a verb meaning "to get up" or "to go up." Rise is an intransitive verb that doesn't need a direct object.

Raise is a verb meaning "to lift" or "to grow." Raise is a transitive verb that requires a direct object.

Examples:

The curtain **rises**.
The girl **raises** her hand.

Raise is a regular verb. Rise is irregular.

Present tense	Past tense	Past participle
rise	rose	has/have/had risen
raise	raised	has/have/had raised

Examples:

The sun **rose** this morning.
The boy **raised** the window higher.

Directions: Write the correct words to complete these sentences.

rises 1. This bread dough rises/raises in an hour.
raise 2. The landlord will rise/raise the rent.
rose 3. The balloon rose/raised into the sky.
raised 4. My sister rose/raised the seat on my bike.
raised 5. The baby rose/raised the spoon to his mouth.
rose 6. The eagle rose/raised out of sight.
raises 7. The farmer rises/raises pigs.
raised 8. The scouts rose/raised the flag.
rose 9. When the fog rose/raised, we could see better.
rose 10. The price of ice cream rose/raised again.
raised 11. The king rose/raised the glass to his lips.
Raise 12. Rise/Raise the picture on that wall higher.

52

"All Right," "All Ready" and "Already"

All right means "well enough" or "very well." Sometimes **all right** is incorrectly spelled. **Alright** is not a word.

Example:

Correct: We'll be all right when the rain stops.
Incorrect: Are you feeling **alright** today?

All ready is an adjective meaning "completely ready."

Already is an adverb meaning "before this time" or "by this time."

Examples:

Are you **all ready** to go?
He was **already** there when I arrived.

Directions: Write the correct words to complete these sentences.

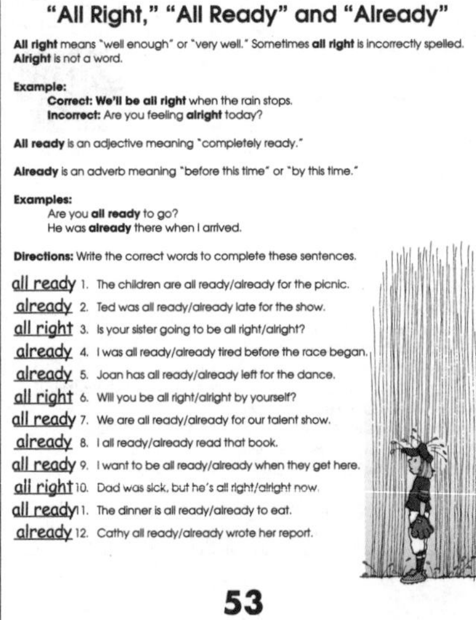

all ready 1. The children are all ready/already for the picnic.
already 2. Ted was all ready/already late for the show.
all right 3. Is your sister going to be all right/alright?
already 4. I was all ready/already tired before the race began.
already 5. Joan has all ready/already left for the dance.
all right 6. Will you be all right/alright by yourself?
all ready 7. We are all ready/already for our talent show.
already 8. I all ready/already read that book.
all ready 9. I want to be all ready/already when they get here.
all right 10. Dad was sick, but he's all right/alright now.
all ready 11. The dinner is all ready/already to eat.
already 12. Cathy all ready/already wrote her report.

53

©2006 Carson-Dellosa Publishing

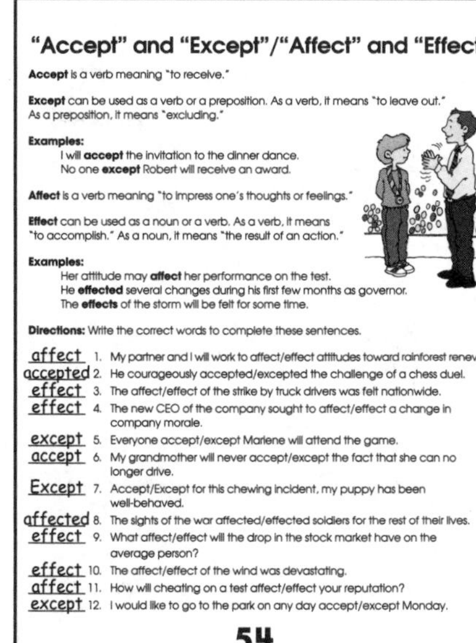

"Accept" and "Except"/"Affect" and "Effect"

Accept is a verb meaning "to receive."

Except can be used as a verb or a preposition. As a verb, it means "to leave out." As a preposition, it means "excluding."

Examples:
I will **accept** the invitation to the dinner dance.
No one **except** Robert will receive an award.

Affect is a verb meaning "to impress one's thoughts or feelings."

Effect can be used as a noun or a verb. As a verb, it means "to accomplish." As a noun, it means "the result of an action."

Examples:
Her attitude may **affect** her performance on the test.
He **effected** several changes during his first few months as governor.
The **effects** of the storm will be felt for some time.

Directions: Write the correct words to complete these sentences.

affect 1. My partner and I will work to affect/effect attitudes toward rainforest renewal.
accepted 2. He courageously accepted/excepted the challenge of a chess duel.
effect 3. The affect/effect of the strike by truck drivers was felt nationwide.
effect 4. The new CEO of the company sought to affect/effect a change in company morale.
except 5. Everyone accept/except Marlene will attend the game.
accept 6. My grandmother will never accept/except the fact that she can no longer drive.
Except 7. Accept/Except for this chewing incident, my puppy has been well-behaved.
affected 8. The sights of the war affected/effected soldiers for the rest of their lives.
effect 9. What affect/effect will the drop in the stock market have on the average person?
effect 10. The affect/effect of the wind was devastating.
affect 11. How will cheating on a test affect/effect your reputation?
except 12. I would like to go to the park on any day accept/except Monday.

54

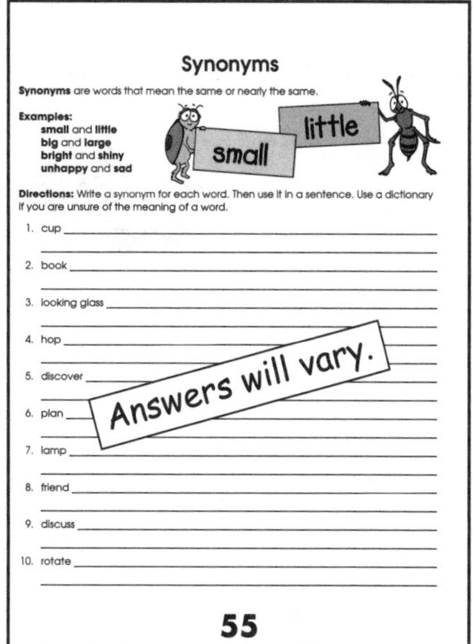

Synonyms

Synonyms are words that mean the same or nearly the same.

Examples:
small and **little**
big and **large**
bright and **shiny**
unhappy and **sad**

Directions: Write a synonym for each word. Then use it in a sentence. Use a dictionary if you are unsure of the meaning of a word.

1. cup
2. book
3. looking glass
4. hop
5. discover
6. plan
7. lamp
8. friend
9. discuss
10. rotate

Answers will vary.

55

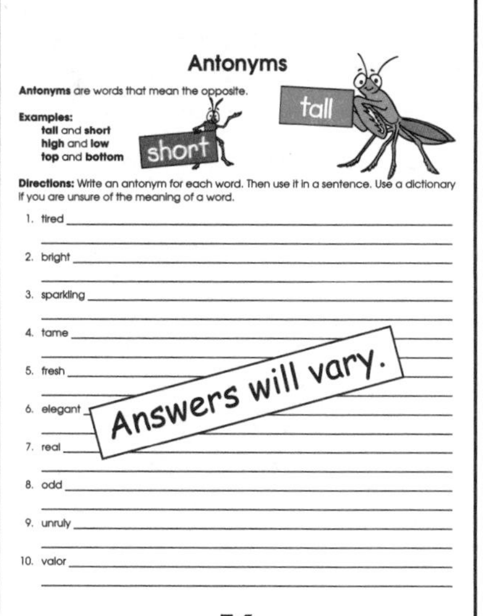

Antonyms

Antonyms are words that mean the opposite.

Examples:
tall and **short**
high and **low**
top and **bottom**

Directions: Write an antonym for each word. Then use it in a sentence. Use a dictionary if you are unsure of the meaning of a word.

1. tired
2. bright
3. sparkling
4. tame
5. fresh
6. elegant
7. real
8. odd
9. unruly
10. valor

Answers will vary.

56

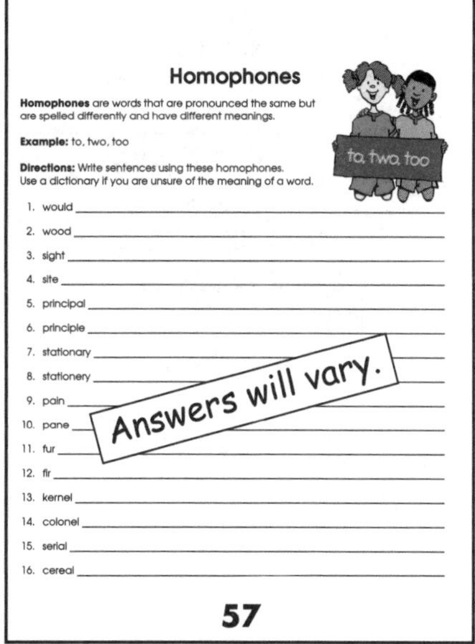

Homophones

Homophones are words that are pronounced the same but are spelled differently and have different meanings.

Example: to, two, too

Directions: Write sentences using these homophones. Use a dictionary if you are unsure of the meaning of a word.

1. would
2. wood
3. sight
4. site
5. principal
6. principle
7. stationary
8. stationery
9. pain
10. pane
11. fur
12. fir
13. kernel
14. colonel
15. serial
16. cereal

Answers will vary.

57

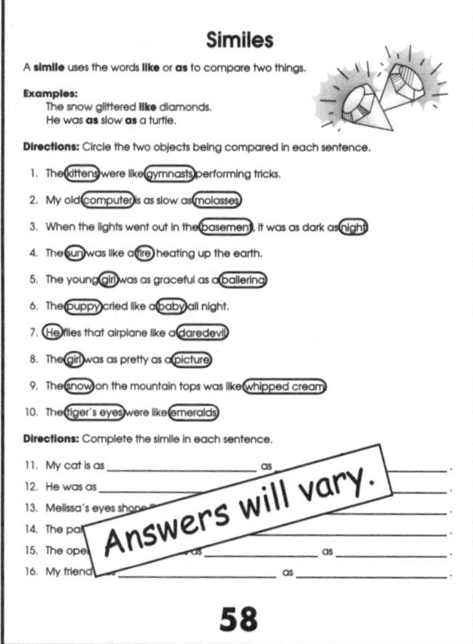

Similes

A **simile** uses the words **like** or **as** to compare two things.

Examples:
The snow glittered **like** diamonds.
He was **as** slow **as** a turtle.

Directions: Circle the two objects being compared in each sentence.

1. The (kittens) were like (gymnasts) performing tricks.
2. My old (computer) is as slow as (molasses).
3. When the lights went out in the (basement), it was as dark as (night).
4. The (sun) was like a (fire) heating up the earth.
5. The young (girl) was as graceful as a (ballerina).
6. The (puppy) cried like a (baby) all night.
7. (He) flies that airplane like a (daredevil).
8. The (girl) was as pretty as a (picture).
9. The (snow) on the mountain tops was like (whipped cream).
10. The (tiger's eyes) were like (emeralds).

Directions: Complete the simile in each sentence.

11. My cat is as ______ as ______.
12. He was as ______.
13. Melissa's eyes shone ______.
14. The pa______.
15. The ope______ as ______ as ______.
16. My friend ______ as ______.

Answers will vary.

58

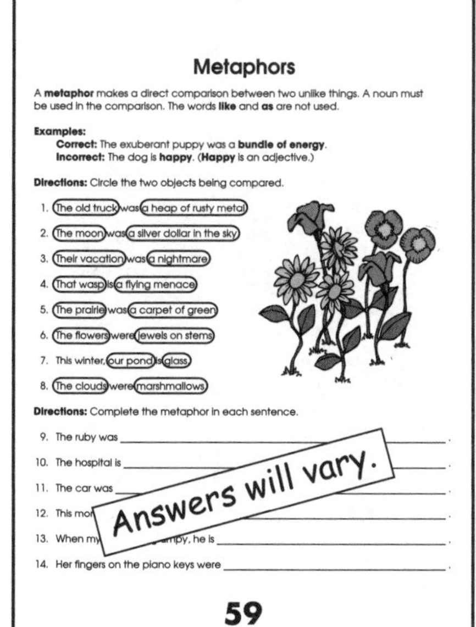

Metaphors

A **metaphor** makes a direct comparison between two unlike things. A noun must be used in the comparison. The words **like** and **as** are not used.

Examples:
Correct: The exuberant puppy was a **bundle of energy**.
Incorrect: The dog is **happy**. (**Happy** is an adjective.)

Directions: Circle the two objects being compared.

1. (The old truck) was (a heap of rusty metal).
2. (The moon) was (a silver dollar in the sky).
3. (Their vacation) was (a nightmare).
4. (That wasp) is (a flying menace).
5. (The prairie) was (a carpet of green).
6. (The flowers) were (jewels on stems).
7. This winter, (our pond) is (glass).
8. (The clouds) were (marshmallows).

Directions: Complete the metaphor in each sentence.

9. The ruby was ______.
10. The hospital is ______.
11. The car was ______.
12. This mo______.
13. When my ______ empty, he is ______.
14. Her fingers on the piano keys were ______.

Answers will vary.

59

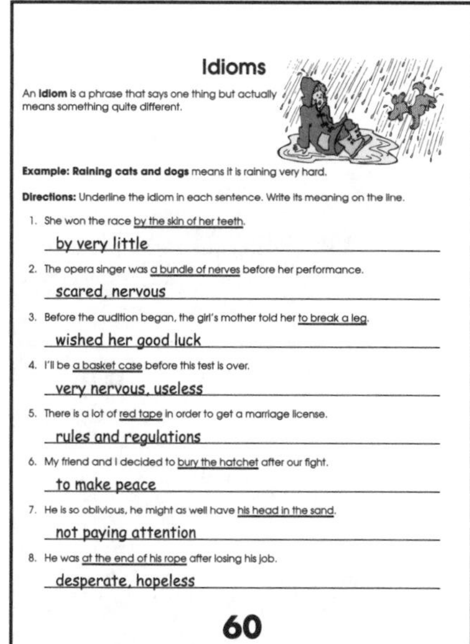

Idioms

An **idiom** is a phrase that says one thing but actually means something quite different.

Example: Raining cats and dogs means it is raining very hard.

Directions: Underline the idiom in each sentence. Write its meaning on the line.

1. She won the race <u>by the skin of her teeth</u>.
by very little
2. The opera singer was <u>a bundle of nerves</u> before her performance.
scared, nervous
3. Before the audition began, the girl's mother told her <u>to break a leg</u>.
wished her good luck
4. I'll be <u>a basket case</u> before this test is over.
very nervous, useless
5. There is a lot of <u>red tape</u> in order to get a marriage license.
rules and regulations
6. My friend and I decided to <u>bury the hatchet</u> after our fight.
to make peace
7. He is so oblivious, he might as well have <u>his head in the sand</u>.
not paying attention
8. He was <u>at the end of his rope</u> after losing his job.
desperate, hopeless

60

©2006 Carson-Dellosa Publishing

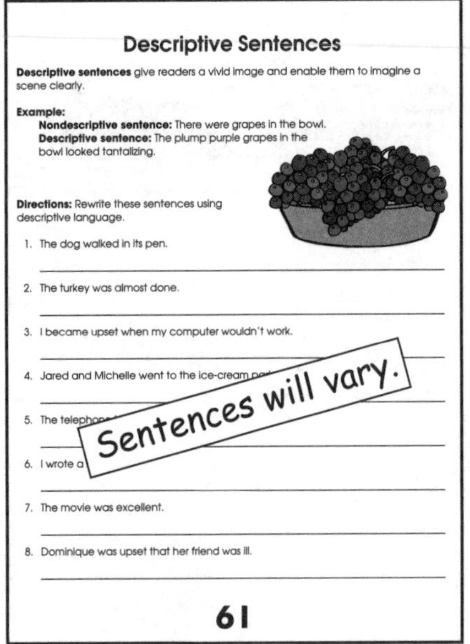

Descriptive Sentences

Descriptive sentences give readers a vivid image and enable them to imagine a scene clearly.

Example:
Nondescriptive sentence: There were grapes in the bowl.
Descriptive sentence: The plump purple grapes in the bowl looked tantalizing.

Directions: Rewrite these sentences using descriptive language.

1. The dog walked in its pen.
2. The turkey was almost done.
3. I became upset when my computer wouldn't work.
4. Jared and Michelle went to the ice-cream par
5. The telephon
6. I wrote a
7. The movie was excellent.
8. Dominique was upset that her friend was ill.

Sentences will vary.

61

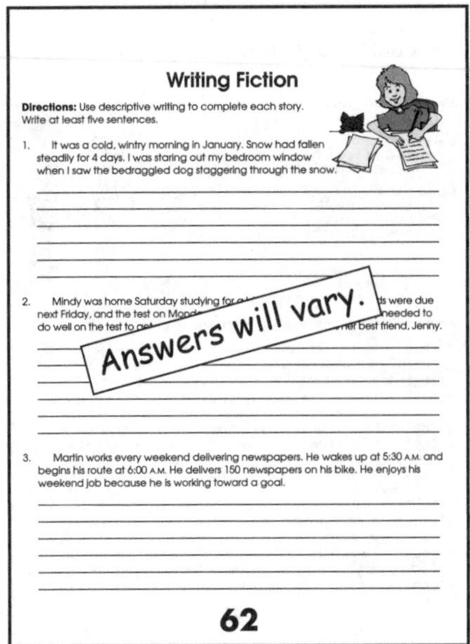

Writing Fiction

Directions: Use descriptive writing to complete each story. Write at least five sentences.

1. It was a cold, wintry morning in January. Snow had fallen steadily for 4 days. I was staring out my bedroom window when I saw the bedraggled dog staggering through the snow.

2. Mindy was home Saturday studying for a … ds were due next Friday, and the test on Mond… needed to do well on the test to ge… her best friend, Jenny.

Answers will vary.

3. Martin works every weekend delivering newspapers. He wakes up at 5:30 A.M. and begins his route at 6:00 A.M. He delivers 150 newspapers on his bike. He enjoys his weekend job because he is working toward a goal.

62

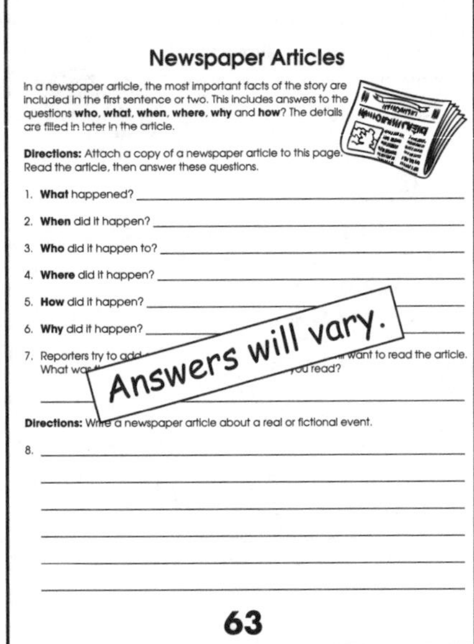

Newspaper Articles

In a newspaper article, the most important facts of the story are included in the first sentence or two. This includes answers to the questions **who**, **what**, **when**, **where**, **why** and **how**? The details are filled in later in the article.

Directions: Attach a copy of a newspaper article to this page. Read the article, then answer these questions.

1. **What** happened?
2. **When** did it happen?
3. **Who** did it happen to?
4. **Where** did it happen?
5. **How** did it happen?
6. **Why** did it happen?
7. Reporters try to add … want to read the article. What wa… you read?

Answers will vary.

Directions: Write a newspaper article about a real or fictional event.

8.

63

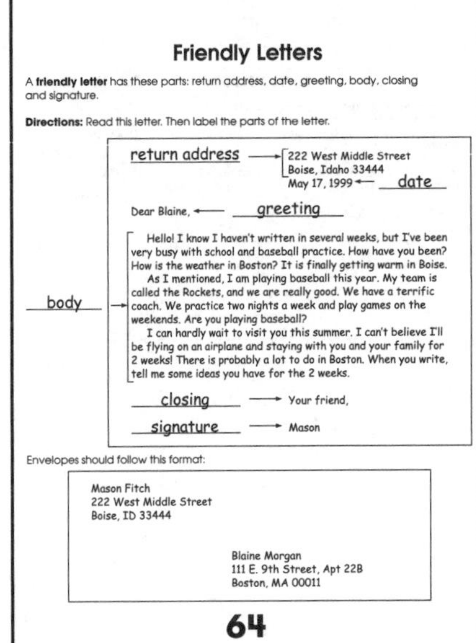

Friendly Letters

A **friendly letter** has these parts: return address, date, greeting, body, closing and signature.

Directions: Read this letter. Then label the parts of the letter.

return address → 222 West Middle Street
Boise, Idaho 33444
May 17, 1999 ← date

Dear Blaine, ← greeting

body →
Hello! I know I haven't written in several weeks, but I've been very busy with school and baseball practice. How have you been? How is the weather in Boston? It is finally getting warm in Boise.
As I mentioned, I am playing baseball this year. My team is called the Rockets, and we are really good. We have a terrific coach. We practice two nights a week and play games on the weekends. Are you playing baseball?
I can hardly wait to visit you this summer. I can't believe I'll be flying on an airplane and staying with you and your family for 2 weeks! There is probably a lot to do in Boston. When you write, tell me some ideas you have for the 2 weeks.

closing → Your friend,
signature → Mason

Envelopes should follow this format:

Mason Fitch
222 West Middle Street
Boise, ID 33444

Blaine Morgan
111 E. 9th Street, Apt 22B
Boston, MA 00011

64

Friendly Letters

Directions: Write a friendly letter. Then address the envelope.

Letters should follow format given.

65

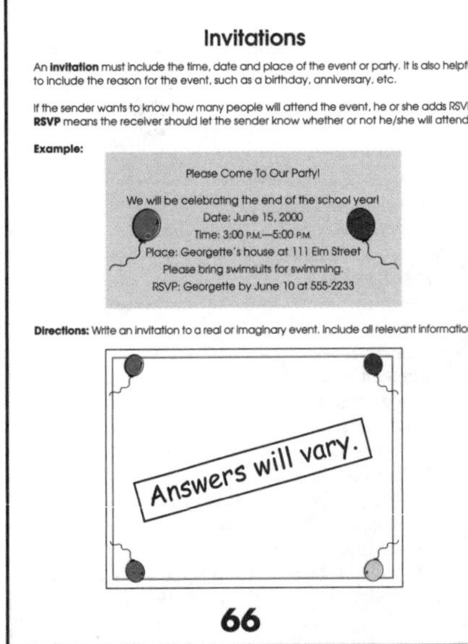

Invitations

An **invitation** must include the time, date and place of the event or party. It is also helpful to include the reason for the event, such as a birthday, anniversary, etc.

If the sender wants to know how many people will attend the event, he or she adds RSVP. **RSVP** means the receiver should let the sender know whether or not he/she will attend.

Example:

Please Come To Our Party!
We will be celebrating the end of the school year!
Date: June 15, 2000
Time: 3:00 P.M.—5:00 P.M.
Place: Georgette's house at 111 Elm Street
Please bring swimsuits for swimming.
RSVP: Georgette by June 10 at 555-2233

Directions: Write an invitation to a real or imaginary event. Include all relevant information.

Answers will vary.

66

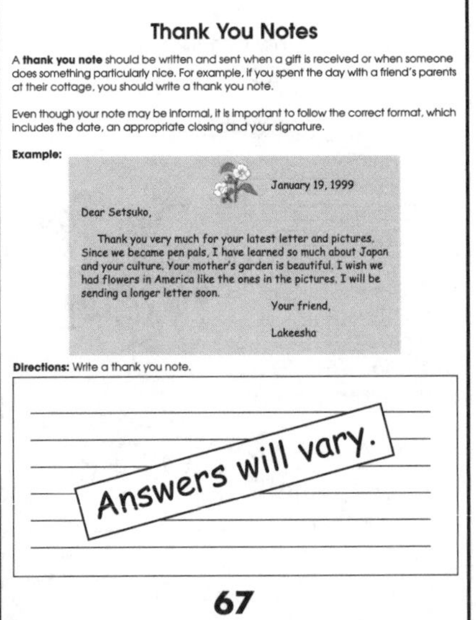

Thank You Notes

A **thank you note** should be written and sent when a gift is received or when someone does something particularly nice. For example, if you spent the day with a friend's parents at their cottage, you should write a thank you note.

Even though your note may be informal, it is important to follow the correct format, which includes the date, an appropriate closing and your signature.

Example:

January 19, 1999

Dear Setsuko,

Thank you very much for your latest letter and pictures. Since we became pen pals, I have learned so much about Japan and your culture. Your mother's garden is beautiful. I wish we had flowers in America like the ones in the pictures. I will be sending a longer letter soon.

Your friend,
Lakeesha

Directions: Write a thank you note.

Answers will vary.

67

 ©2006 Carson-Dellosa Publishing

Haiku

Haiku is a form of unrhymed Japanese poetry. Haiku have three lines. The first line has five syllables, the second line has seven syllables and the third line has five syllables.

Example:

The Fall

Leaves fall from the trees.
Do they want to leave their home?
They float on the breeze.

Directions: Write a haiku about nature. Write the title on the first line. Then illustrate your haiku.

Nature ______________________

Poems should follow format.

____

____

68

Lantern

Lantern is another type of five-line Japanese poetry. It takes the shape of a Japanese lantern. Each line must contain the following number of syllables.

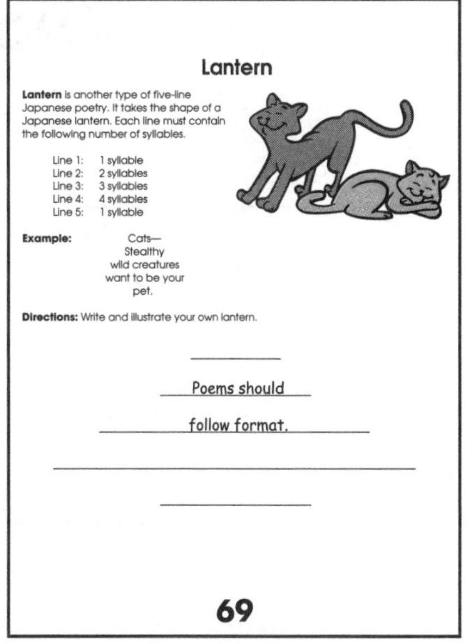

Line 1: 1 syllable
Line 2: 2 syllables
Line 3: 3 syllables
Line 4: 4 syllables
Line 5: 1 syllable

Example:

Cats—
Stealthy
wild creatures
want to be your
pet.

Directions: Write and illustrate your own lantern.

______

Poems should

follow format.

____

____

69

©2006 Carson-Dellosa Publishing

Notes